Yellowstone Autumn

American Lives

Series editor: Tobias Wolff

W. D. Wetherell

Yellowstone Autumn

A Season of Discovery in a Wondrous Land

University of Nebraska Press • Lincoln and London

© 2009
by the
Board of Regents
of the
University of Nebraska
All rights reserved
Manufactured in the
United States of America
∞
Library of Congress
Cataloging-in-Publication Data
Wetherell, W. D.,
Yellowstone autumn:
a season of discovery in
a wondrous land
/ W. D. Wetherell.
p.   cm.
— (American lives)
ISBN 978-0-8032-1130-8
(cloth : alk. paper)
1. Wetherell, W. D., 1948–
2. Yellowstone National Park
—Biography.
I. Title.

PS3573.E9248Z46 2009
813'.54—dc22
[B]
2008036832

Set in Scala by Bob Reitz.
Designed by R. W. Boeche.

For Celeste, Erin, and Matthew

Contents

One

WHAT KIND OF MAN wants to be alone on his birthday? Wants to be lonely on that day. Wants to be homesick. Wants to go without wishes for a good one, jokes about getting up there, cracks about being over the hill. Wants to avoid presents, cards, cakes, candles. Wants to go someplace where no one knows him or cares about him or even notices him, hopes to find in this solitude a blinding flash of insight into his existential condition, a serenity that will see him safely through the coming year, a solace he can draw upon like an unlimited savings account, a wisdom that will make him the envy of all his friends. Wants, at the very minimum, to catch a trophy brown trout of such size, strength, and vibrancy that it temporarily reconciles him to life, the late middle part of it anyway, the upcoming installment in a trial by existence that wasn't getting any easier in this his fifty-sixth year.

There are plenty who *have* to be alone on their birthday; choice doesn't enter into it. In making my resolution I thought a lot about those poor souls who would give anything to have the family I have, and it made me hesitate. You often get what you wish for, especially on birthdays, and asking for solitude tempts a mordant power that is ever ready to oblige. I had been alone on my thirtieth birthday and not because I was indulging a whim. Alone, as in depressed, suicidal, bewildered, suffering the illusion that in a world of the interconnected I was the only one who had failed to catch on. I can remember that feeling all too clearly—what real solitude is like, how easily it can ensnare a person, how difficult it can be to break free.

So I wasn't going to brag about my intention, far better just to slink away before anyone even noticed I was gone. To my family I tried explaining as best I could my more comprehensible motives. I'd had a difficult professional year in which luck seemed to have turned against me, and I needed to do something dramatic to change the run of play. I wanted (reason number two) to commemorate a birthday I saw as a landmark, the real big 5–5, not the phony big 5–0 that I had passed in a breeze. I wanted to get out from under things for a few weeks—the weight of routine, the burden of responsibilities, the settled groove a life sinks into. I needed to see things from the side, edge-on, from an entirely new perspective I couldn't manage at home. I wanted to test my eyes on a different landscape, sharpen my vision by having to rely on my seeing alone.

I wanted to accomplish all those things, take three weeks like Thoreau had taken his twenty-six months (in the inflated press of modern times, three weeks alone now is roughly commensurate to one year alone in 1845). But since these motives are difficult to explain, I usually announced another one, that was easier for people to understand: "The fishing is supposed to be great in Yellowstone in the fall. Spawning browns. I've always wanted to give it a try."

This is the nice thing about having an avocation you pursue

passionately—it becomes your alibi for everything. For most
people, trout fishing is a much handier motive than philosophy.
"You're going fishing? I envy you." That's the kind of response I
was, uh, angling for, and for the most part that's what I got.

My daughter, Erin, age seventeen, was much shrewder; her
comment cut right to the heart of the matter, and I didn't have a
snappy comeback. "Alone? On your birthday? You'll be homesick,
you'll be home in two days."

She was probably right—but what I couldn't explain to her
was that I needed to remind myself how good my life was, how
far I had come since that thirtieth birthday alone. And even this
was minor compared to my prime motive. My prime reason for
wanting to be alone in Yellowstone National Park on my fifty-fifth
birthday was to discover why I needed so badly to be alone in Yellowstone National Park on my fifty-fifth birthday.

Yellowstone, after all, was not the obvious choice. Anyone wanting to commemorate a big birthday might prefer going someplace
exotic, backpacking on Baffin Island, say, or fly-fishing for those
monster sea-run browns in Tierra del Fuego. I thought about this,
but then decided (prodded by my bank account) that such a place
would be *too* exotic—that there I would have no frame of reference
within which I could begin to puzzle things out. This was going
to be my year of paying attention, my year of slowing down—and
tundra, exotica, weirdness, seemed the wrong way to start.

But Yellowstone can be a weird place, too, with its signature
blend of the beautiful and the bizarre. I'd been there several times
before. My first visit was in 1988—timed so that I arrived at the
peak of the great fires, when two-thirds of the park was aflame.
I've wondered over the years if this wasn't one of the reasons I fell
in love with it so rapidly—that when I first saw the park, it was

very close to disappearing. The great clouds of smoke; the sweet, inescapable smell of burning pine; the long line of firefighters waiting at pay phones to call home to say they were okay; the black, steaming embers I had to tiptoe around in order to fish. I sensed an awesomeness inside an awesomeness I couldn't penetrate—and when I left, defeated in my effort to see more than a fraction, I couldn't wait to come back.

Yellowstone is purest America, Wonderland, the country's least-known best-known place. Millions go there, but very few *see* it; the normal park stay is less than twenty-four hours, and only 2 percent of visitors ever leave the park roads. People know about the geysers, remember their parents' stories about feeding the bears, have heard horror stories about the crowds, and most seem content to leave it at that; in the contemporary American imagination it's become a place that was long since tamed, Jellystone National Park, with photogenic bison, adorable rangers, and Old Faithful.

The Yellowstone I had come to know is entirely different—a place where with only the slightest amount of effort you can be alone in one of the most magnificent and unspoiled landscapes in the world. For Yellowstone even now is *the* classic American place—and a shot of pure, classic America is something I badly needed after the year we lovers of the country had been through. With all that happened, ever since . . . and you can insert your own favorite atrocity here . . . I'd still managed to cling to an unreasoned, instinctive, gut-level patriotism that makes the manufactured, flag-waving version seem puny. In my genes, in all our genes, is a chemical signal that is not quite extinct, a pulse that awakens in us, give it half a chance—the original awe and wonder our ancestors felt when they first came face to face with the continent's splendors. Every new outrage, every new shabbiness, each new instance of aggression, and the gene grows fainter, yet in Yellowstone the wonder comes alive again, the love for the land that can be so overpowering it makes me want to sob.

Yellowstone has always been one of the places where writers go for meaning, as in, What is the *meaning* of Yellowstone? Yes, I told myself, in planning all the details, I'll take a crack at that—and maybe there will be enough meaning left over that I can apply some to myself.

For reading material, I brought along some accounts by early travelers to Yellowstone—the ones who were afraid of being branded as outrageous liars if they wrote sober, matter-of-fact accounts of what they had seen. These narratives all begin with the long, hard slog to reach the park. Reading these, I couldn't bring myself to complain about the plane ride west to Bozeman. Yes, it was a good flight, there were no major foul-ups, I was frisked going through security by an unusually polite and apologetic guard, we flew right over a brilliantly shiny Toronto, and later the pilot obligingly lowered a wing so we could see the furrowed hillside site of Custer's Last Stand.

There was some down time in Minneapolis between flights and I noticed something as I waited. I noticed that when you reach my age, no one notices you. Seniors, yes, they're quick to be scooped up by those golf carts and whisked to their proper gate; kids, too—there are always people on the lookout for lost kids. The teenagers and the twentysomethings check each other out and casually preen . . . which leaves middle-aged people to cope on their own. No one expects a fuss out of us, no one ogles us or pities us, we're pretty much part of the plastic.

But I'm noticing the late middle-agers, even if no one else is, men a little older than I am, men in their late fifties or early sixties. I can't remember doing this since I was twelve—looking at older males to find a role model I could emulate. There are a surprisingly large number of men to choose from, a good many traveling alone. The businessmen I quickly skip, finding them too haggard-looking, too predictable; the paunchy men a little ahead of their wives on the moving sidewalk I skip over as well. But there are others, comfortable, fit-looking men who sometimes carry briefcases, but are more apt to be toting fly rods or tennis rackets or even fairly thick books. They're a damn-fine-looking bunch; they tend to be tanned, tend to wear chinos, tend to look like football refs. The ones I stare at longest seem marked by a generous kind of sophistication (they can talk with anybody), and a relaxed sort of acceptance; they're comfortable with themselves, but far from smug. Role models? The kind of man I'd like to be in ten years' time? Well, maybe, maybe not, but it's interesting to catch myself looking.

The only other part of the trip worth mentioning is the unbelievable miracle of it, something the unsophisticated nineteenth-century hick in me can never get over. I wake up just before dawn in rural New England, walk to our window that faces east, see in the moonlight the lenticular cloud that drapes itself over the wooded slope of our local mountain, then go to bed that same night in a cabin facing Mount Evarts, the castle-like rampart that seals off Yellowstone's northwest corner, watching the same moon apply the same milky whitewash against an entirely different texture. The same day! It's a hard concept to get your mind around—so hard it made me restless, and about midnight, to convince myself I was really there, I threw on my jacket and went outside.

I was there all right. Yellowstone, by god. The Mammoth terraces, the reek of sulfur, elk droppings squishing underfoot. I walked gingerly over to the old parade ground, crossed to the middle, stood there looking up at the bright red eye of Mars (at its closest approach to earth in centuries), then turned to face the ghostly steam wafting off the bone-colored terraces behind me.

Wrapped around me with the moonlight was a silence that at first seemed total (and why, I wondered then and later, is silence in Yellowstone *more* silent than silence in New Hampshire?). But I was wrong on this; my ears simply hadn't adapted yet to this new, richer, more pregnant kind of ether, and after a few minutes my hearing, like my vision, started to catch up.

Faint at first, like a distant radio station that isn't quite tuned in, then much sharper, came the sound of wolves, frantically howling, yipping and barking. Closer, but just as wild, was the sound of elk bugling, showing off for their harems, warning off rivals, enjoying, it's easy to imagine, their liberation from muteness that only comes once a year. Earlier, I'd seen bulls grazing on the lawn outside the old officers' quarters; there's a ventriloquistic quality to the sound they make, and when you look at the animal that's emitting the sound, it looks like it must be coming from somewhere else.

Now in the darkness, listening intently, I tried coming up with a better description of what I was hearing. There is definitely a bugle note in an elk's call—a bugle as played by a kid in summer camp who's got lots of wind, but not much lip. There's also something birdlike about it, a lonesome bird, something on the order of a loon. Add a horse's whinny—a kind of pathetic and wistful clumsiness of expression, as if the elk, though trying its best, regrets not making the sound sweeter. If you had to guess, not knowing what the sound came from, you might think it was a squeaky pipe organ played at its highest pitch. Pipe organ, horse whinny, bugle, loon. Blend all these and you can start to imagine the kind of primal thrill it must create in a female elk.

But say one thing for it—it's one of the few sounds in nature worth traveling two thousand miles to hear. When the chill finally got to me and I went back to my cabin, the sound was even louder, the air absolutely lousy with elk lust. But that's not a bad thing for a man my age to fall asleep to after crossing the continent in a single bound, not a bad thing at all.

A man my age. How curious that the words come to me this way now. Another taunting symptom of late middle age—and I seem to be on the lookout for these everywhere. There's a new kind of brooding I've been doing half-heartedly at home, and one of my purposes in visiting Yellowstone was to find the time and space to brood more explicitly, letting my moodiness have its head. Any year is a journey, of course, but this upcoming year loomed as a harder, more significant journey than the others in my life, so there was all the more reason to emerge from it with a semi-lucid account. The event-crammed, seemingly endless years of middle age, with luck, can seem like a prolonged voyage along a well-marked coast—hard, sure, stormy, often, but with those reassuring beacons, lighthouses and channel markers to help one sail on. Late middle age promises to be, as I prepare to set out, an entirely different kind of voyage, one that takes me well out of sight of land, amid icebergs and reefs, tsunamis and williwaws, with no navigational aids or buoys, and no chance of rescue.

While there are many memoirs of youth and aspiration, and—a new fashion—many accounts of midlife crises, as well as reminiscences of old people summing up their lives, there are hardly any memoirs written of late-middle age. How-to books, yes—users' manuals by pop psychologists who usually advise you to set goals and draw up lists. Except for these, the sixth decade of life, the fifties, represent a largely unknown zone, a decade you're expected to barge through with your mouth stoically shut. The heroes of the great American novels are jaded, used-up men at thirty; there *are* second acts in American lives (Fitzgerald was wrong on this), but no one is interested in watching past the first.

It's always been an oddly silent, under-reported decade—and yet, judging by the years I've already had of it, it can be the most testing decade of all, real crunch time when it comes to the trial-by-existence we all undergo, the decade when a life draws to the point where there are simply no more Yet here we are, men and women both, suddenly dealing with the most profound and troubling physical and emotional changes since puberty, and so who we are, rather than being a finished product, becomes, yet again, a work in progress.

Late middle age is not the end of the journey, far from it, and people that age can experience despair not unlike that which a young person feels when they're faced with the daunting task of making a place for themselves in a largely indifferent world. Here's a quote from someone whose life was a real journey, not just a metaphoric one—Roald Amundsen, the first person to reach the South Pole. At age fifty-four, he's experiencing a typical late-middle-age moment, albeit with a twist, he's lamenting the fact that he can't find any backers for a new expedition, this one to fly over the North Pole in a dirigible:

As I sat in my room at the Waldorf Astoria, it seemed to me as if the future had closed solidly against me, and that my career as an

explorer had come to an inglorious end. Courage, will power, indomi-
table faith—these qualities had carried me through many adventures
and to many achievements. Now even their merits seemed of no avail.
I was nearer to black despair than ever before in my 54 years of life.

The future had closed solidly against me. That's what an ardent,
frustrated twenty-year-old is supposed to feel, not a successful
man in his mid-fifties. I read this passage five times when I first
came across it, put the book down, went outside to chop wood,
came back and read it three more times. This feels like the same
predicament that has taken hold of me at precisely Amundsen's
age—that all those virtues that have gotten me this far in the journey, scraps of seamanship, rough- and-ready navigational talents,
a gritty kind of stamina, are suddenly of no use whatsoever in the
journey toward the next stage of life. Youthful ardor? Ardor of the
Amundsen kind? Yes, it's great while it lasts, and it can last for a
surprisingly long time, but what happens when it ends?

We hear a lot of talk about midlife crises, but these are fash-
ionable, even expected, for people age forty or forty-five. If I ever
experienced one it happened during the night and I slept right
through it. My forties were busy years, successful ones, and there
was never a point where I felt the need (let alone the ability) to
slow time down the way I intended to slow it down on this trip;
the family-friends-career current was sweeping me along, sure,
but for the most part it was roughly the direction I wished to be
carried.

Now I'm not sure where the current is taking me, feel puzzled
by this, even panicky, so I spend an inordinate amount of time
emotionally flailing about—or, in reaction to the fatigue of this,
passively treading water. The truth is, the past year had been

testing. A sudden roadblock in my career (and a pothole in my vocation's future), a declining family income at the very time the demands on that income are highest, some health concerns, even—and you have to live in rural New England to appreciate the weight of this—the coldest, longest winter of our twenty-five years here, followed by the wettest, gloomiest summer. Add to these the heartbreaking spectacle of the country I love suddenly running amok, and it was not a year I'd care to repeat.

Certainly, the coming year is going to be full of changes whether I welcome them or not. My son, Matthew, at thirteen, is entering the crucial years of puberty; later in the year he will be leaving our cozy local grade school for the challenge of an aggressively competitive high school in the neighboring town. My daughter, Erin, will be graduating from high school and beginning her first year in college, assuming we ever complete this nerve-wracking search for which one to attend. My father, nearing ninety, beset by handicaps that make mine seem puny, is faced with leaving the home he's lived in for forty-six years. All of which means I'm a charter member of the sandwich generation, though at times the responsibility makes it seem less like being squished between bread slices than being pressed between the jaws of a vise.

My marriage, as always, is a constant tug-of-war—the tug on one side being the life Celeste and I have managed to work out for ourselves over the course of twenty years, the tug on the other side being the pandemic virus (there is no other word) of divorce, which spreads through our culture, through our town . . . yes, here it comes now, working its way door to door . . . so all who value their marriage as we do can't help feeling that in the absence of a miraculous inoculation their marriage may be the next to become sick. Add to this all my emotional failings (so far yet from the serenity I thought I'd have gained by now; too boyishly innocent, too easily hurt, for a person my age, in my profession) and the physical changes I see in myself, which are the most extreme since puberty, and it equals a year that promises to pose a unique set of challenges, with plenty of everyday drama, as a man and his family seek to be true to themselves in what are, in what always are, perilous times.

I realize that there are many other people currently embarked on a similar journey. Late middle age can sometimes be lonely and a solo voyage, but a more apt analogy might be to an enormous armada of ships, often invisible to each other in the fog, moving in parallel. Through a trick of demographic history, a vastly larger than average number of babies were born in America during the ten years following World War Two. Many people had delayed having families because of the war, others had held off because of Depression-induced fears that they wouldn't be able to adequately care for them. The intersection of a large supply of prospective parents, for whom the biological clock was rapidly ticking, with a large supply of prospective parents suddenly very confident about the future meant—along with all the other enormous implications for our society and culture—that in the first years of the twenty-first century there would be a huge number of adults in this country very close to either side of their fifty-fifth birthday, including me.

Which brings up a question of definition. To young people, people in their fifties are old, end of story. To octogenarians, someone my age is a brash youngster, and they don't want to hear any complaints. Split the difference and you can label us middle-aged, but that's too broad a term to span many real differences. Late middle age, a person's fifties, are much different than a early middle age, a person's thirties. Then, too, as with puberty, the aging process varies tremendously from individual to individual (and when I say "aging," I mean aging well just as much as I mean aging badly). And yet my gut instinct is that the border is very precise—that someone fifty-four is middle-aged; that someone fifty-five is *late*-middle-aged. (With increasing life spans, seniors running wild, people talk about sixty being "the new forty," but if you play around with this scale, eighteen-year-olds are newborns.)

Arbitrary? You bet. I'm drawing lines, me who hates to draw lines, but there you are. We fifty-four-year-eleven-month-twelve-day-olds tend to be melodramatic. Whether fifty-five turns out to be a cliff over which I tumble, a trampoline from which I bounce up and down in pretty much the same place, or a springboard launching me toward better things (toward serenity? generosity? acceptance?) I will soon discover, and yet the fact that something new and different is taking hold of me is—from this cabin where I lie awake brooding—indisputable. Late middle age is where the young part of you and the old part stand tightly back to back, and what is good about it and what is bad comes from their alternately comforting and irritating negotiations.

Up early in the morning, a quick bite to eat in the cafeteria, a bag lunch packed, then out I drive on the Mammoth–Tower Road, exhilarated from being in the exact place on the planet I want to be at absolutely the right moment.

Yellowstone labors under a burden that would sink a lesser place: everyone who visits here expects to be enchanted immediately. The good news is that, yes, you come upon enchantment very quickly, especially in the morning when you're apt to have

the road to yourself, and the landscape comes dramatically alive
under the sunrise. Take my drive from Mammoth out to the Lamar
Valley. You follow the golden ramparts of Mount Evarts, crane your
head down to see the Gardner River racing through its canyon far
below the first high bridge, have the shadows come back again as
the road pinches against the cliffs of Lava Canyon, emerge onto
the rolling, sage-covered meadows of the Blacktail Deer plateau,
pass several old lakes, see to your left the tight, hidden folds of the
Black Canyon of the Yellowstone, the wooded right- to-left green
slant of Hellroaring Creek, cross the surging Yellowstone on the
Cooke City bridge, then follow Specimen Ridge with its wildlife
and petrified trees before coming out . . . as the sun pours down
full strength . . . into the overwhelming beauty of the Lamar Valley, America's Serengeti, with wolves and buffalo and antelope
and the whole Yellowstone nine yards, a basin of magnificence
backed up by the Beartooth and Absarokas.

Not bad for a forty-minute drive—and I didn't see another car
until I came to Tower Junction. The sun was in my face most of
the way, so I stopped frequently and waited for it to rise higher.
I'd heard stories about snowstorms in autumn shutting the park
down, had come equipped with layer upon layer of GORE-TEX
and fleece, but it would be a while before I broke them out. The
weather that first day was the same that I had for my first two
weeks. Temperature in the high seventies; zero humidity; a perfectly cloudless sky; hardly any wind; a sun that at the high altitude
burned through all the sunscreen I splashed on. It was exhilarating weather, desert-like in its clarity, the famous Rocky Mountain
high—lousy for fishing, but stimulating all to hell.

The only definite sign of fall was the golden aspen trees, which,
with the sun pouring through their branches, were absolutely at

their peak. They grow in well-spaced groves that stand out even more noticeably than maples do in New England; what's more, they have no foliage competition, except for the willows along the creeks (and, outside the park, the yellow cottonwoods). Aspen tend to be flame-shaped in silhouette; their leaves give the impression of wanting to fall *up*, to sail skyward, unlike maple leaves which ponderously want to go down. They're one of the stars in the park in autumn, and if I passed a grove near the road it was sure to be surrounded by photographers trying to come up with those classic cliché shots you see when September rolls around on western calendars.

I did my share of aspen watching during my visit, but on that first morning I was on the lookout for one tree in particular, of another species, a lodgepole pine. And there it was on the burned-over ridge north of Tower Junction, just where it had been the last time and the time before that. The scars from the '88 fires have healed remarkably in the years since, with the green fuzz that took hold almost immediately afterward now grown into teenaged trees taller than I am. The ridge I was looking at had been burned over entirely, being dotted with black limbless trunks that made it look like Verdun circa 1916, a spiky forest of ugly charcoal. But there on the very crest of the ridge . . . and I had spotted this first on a visit in 1990 . . . was a single mature and flourishing pine, one that had survived when every tree on either side of it in a radius of three miles had caught fire and burned.

It was still there, I'm glad to report, though it wasn't easy to pick out, with the new green slowly reclaiming the ridge. A younger man (I told myself) wouldn't have seen my pine, it's just not the kind of exception his eye would be sensitive to; an older man probably would have seen only dead trees and turned away a little sad. And

how old was my tree anyway? Fifty-four? Fifty-five? Old enough
to teach some lessons, at any rate. Life amid the ruins. Surviving
when all around had gone down in flames. Showing the random
play of chance and how it can exalt as well as crush. I spent a long
time sitting on the warm hood of my car staring up at the pine,
thinking long, deep, Yellowstone thoughts. It's a remarkable tree.
A survivor tree. My favorite tree in the entire park.

The nice thing about driving early is that you miss most of the
elk jams, where RV drivers suddenly slam on the brakes in the
middle of the road and disgorge camera-toting occupants who
immediately surround an embarrassed squirrel (quite often it's
squirrels), while behind them other RVs screech to a stop and
disgorge similar creatures, backing things up.

This time of morning, this time of year, you're more apt to come
across serious wildlife spotters, the ones who are careful to use
the pullouts, and sit there behind spotting scopes keeping one
particular moose or eagle in view for hours at a time. They're a
sociable bunch; you see them sharing coffee with fellow spotters,
and they're quick to let newcomers squint through their scopes.
Seeing a pod of them is usually a good sign that a wolf is in sight,
sometimes even a grizz.

The Lamar Ranger Station is a favorite location for wildlife
watchers, with its expansive views of the valley leading up to the
Mirror Plateau. Today they had spotted a herd of antelope, which I
could see when I parked one pullout down—gentle whitish things
clustered within a bend of the river, keyed up like debutantes at a
ball, watching us with as much interest as we observed them.

I'd like to think I could someday be content with just watching
nature from a distance, making no disturbance at all, but I'm not

there yet—I still need a closer, more involved kind of engagement. In pursuit of such, I opened the trunk, strung together my fly rod, donned my new Patagonia waders, pulled on my fishing vest, stuffed snacks in my pockets, applied sunscreen—busied myself with the fly-fisher's equivalent of primping.

For my first morning's fishing, I chose the spot where the Lamar is farthest from the road, a sign of continued youth, I told myself—that distance from the road is still a plus in my eye, not a minus. It was an easy enough walk through the usual mix of sage, buffalo pies and willow. The Lamar is a spate river, which means it has a broad, scoured floodplain that becomes rockier the closer to its banks you come. It means, more to the point, that the trout roam the river in unpredictable ways, so you have to do a lot of walking and squinting to locate where they are.

The minutiae of an angling day are a fascinating subject, but, to paraphrase Mark Twain, only fascinating to those who find it fascinating. Suffice it to say, I had a hard time conjuring trout from the trout-shaped rocks, an even harder time getting those I located to rise to my fly. A good cutthroat lazily swirled toward my rubber-legged Kaufmann stimulator, but I was too tender with him and he broke free. The sun rose to full strength pretty fast, and its brightness didn't help. I was soon in that familiar self-defeating mood: wherein, not getting much action, I stopped paying attention and missed random strikes.

I fished hard most of the morning, then sudden bagged it; there's not much shade along the Lamar, and I have a redhead's sensitivity to the sun. I hiked back to the car, then drove east past the channel where the Lamar is joined by the smaller Soda Butte. The trout proved even scarcer here than on the Lamar, but it was more my kind of water, and after a half mile of careful wading

I found what turned out to be the best cutthroat of my entire trip: a twenty-one-inch male, with that beautiful buttery copper color along the flanks, and the telltale flash of pinkish orange below the gills. It was an extraordinarily large fish in water so thin. I played him slowly and carefully, then, once he was in my net, flailed about like a madman to pull my camera out, lay him beside my rod on the bank, snap a picture and return him to the water unharmed.

What was a fish that size doing so high up the river? I didn't find any more like him, though I caught some decent fish in the pockets and pools of Ice Box Canyon. After that, I tried the Lamar lower down, in its own dark canyon, then, needing fish which were easier to catch, switched to my lightest fly rod, stuffed my pockets with grasshopper imitations, hiked for a mile down Blacktail Deer Creek, and fished my way back to the road, catching two or three brook trout—yes, New England brook trout—in every pool.

I enjoyed this immensely; enjoyed the miniaturization of the whole Yellowstone experience, the sneaking around the willows from pool to pool, the generous willingness of the trout to play along, the connection that came between us via the supple inter-mediary of my fly rod. (And this was one of the reasons I had come to Yellowstone alone; none of my fishing pals enjoy small-stream fishing as much as I do.) After the classically western expanse of the morning's fishing, this was a more intimate experience, and reminded me what the Green Mountains streams were like in Vermont once upon a fast disappearing time. If anything, these trout in their spawning colors seemed brighter and richer than any I had caught at home—their copper so intense, the coral decorations so blinding, I couldn't hold one in my hand without blinking.

After a while, I didn't bother trying to hook them, just enjoyed the way they appeared out of nowhere to attack the grasshopper, these little bubbling upsurges that always startled me, no matter how many I saw.

It was late by the time I quit; I drove back to my cabin at Mammoth worn out from a long day. With the weather being so perfect, there were more visitors around than I expected; seeing the families having fun, eating dinner together, pointing at the elk, made me homesick—but maybe that wasn't so bad, to still feel anything at my age that was identical to what I felt when I was twelve.

I went into the Mammoth store, found a pint bottle of bourbon called Old Faithful. It was cheap stuff, raw—had they included geyser water in the blend?—but it eased away the homesickness. I shared some with my neighbors as we sat on our joint porch watching Mars rise over Mount Evarts. They were my age, they loved the park as I did, and we clicked immediately. They were curious—about my fishing, but most of all about why I wanted to be alone on my birthday. I decided, as we drank, that during the rest of my life, my attention and interest would go strictly to those people my age who were still, whatever else they were, *curious*—that the only fiftysomethings worth bothering with were those who had survived a half century with their curiosity intact.

I wished them goodnight and went back to my cabin, but not yet to sleep. I wanted to start in on another resolution, which was to spend the evenings trying to put my mind around some of the big things I had come here to tackle.

But it's hard to be profound on cue. I thought deep thoughts all right, lying on my bed in the soft yellow of the porch light, sipping Old Faithful, listening to the giggles of children being tucked into bed and the love calls of elk. I thought how deep the

pain was in my knees, backs and shoulders. Before the trip, I had
resolved not to fish myself into my usual stupor, and here I had
done exactly that on my very first day. "Fishing hard" is the term
the macho boys use to denote such a day; not sitting on a bank
dangling a worm into a stream, but actively hunting, searching,
wading, for twelve hours at a stretch.

Thanks to aspirin I could still fish hard—but what of it? I had
noticed this in myself for a few years now, a tendency to swing
between moods wherein I would tell myself I was getting too soft,
and moods where I would decide the opposite, that I'm too hard
on myself, need to ease up. I had talked with enough friends to
know that this kind of back and forth was one of the real identify-
ing traits of late middle age. Some people, the self-damning kind,
swing too far toward the first, and others, the slackers, may give
in too soon to the second, which leaves a few of us trying to keep
a sensible equilibrium.

Living in my town is a group of men my age who commemorate
the summer solstice by hiking the entire Presidential Range in
the White Mountains in one day—twenty-two miles of the most
rugged terrain in the Northeast. They used to invite me to come,
but what's the point of such a test? To prove that you can still do
everything you could do when you were twenty-five? Yes, there is
a certain splendid defiance in attempting such marathons (which
have their sexual and gustatory equivalents), but they can also hide
changes that are real, imminent, not to be denied. All these tests
are ones you are soon going to fail, and the real tests you should
probably be getting ready for are the moral tests of late middle
age, which are an entirely different proposition.

Men my age run marathons, and so do women. Both sexes kick
against time with surgery or makeup. I don't mean to sneer at

them, a little defiance is fine, but I sense that clinging to youth so desperately is not right for me, not quite my style. If I needed to test anything during my stay in the park, it wasn't my hardness but my softness—my ability to open myself to beauty and splendor and all those things hard fishing, hard drinking, hard screwing can rush you past. And so for the short term . . . as I lay there writing in my notebook . . . I resolved to slack off more during the rest of the trip, to be easier on myself, to sit on the bank and smell the flowers (well, enjoy the aspen), not deny certain important lessons my joints were trying to teach me. Easy does it, fella. Not a bad motto, and I wrote it down in big letters.

When you enter the park, the packet of information the ranger hands you has a yellow paper with a cartoon of a charging buffalo butting a man hard enough to knock him over. The National Park Service, having experimented over the years, has found that the cartoon is a much more effective warning than the caution they used to give out which had no illustration. (But not totally effective; during my time in Yellowstone, two middle-aged men approaching bulls for close-up photos were gored.)

Bison, grizzlies, horny elk or rutting moose, the earth giving way beneath your feet as you approach a thermal feature, or—a real concern now among geologists—the risk that the entire Yellowstone caldera will undergo an enormous volcanic eruption in the very near future: these are all dangers to be respected. But in my visits to the park I've found that by far the greatest danger here is letting all the irony get you. Ironic National Park—that's what you'll see of it, if you don't keep a lid on your cynicism. All those monstrous rvs big enough to transport a regiment, or the suvs, which out west apparently pass for subcompacts. The highway cloverleaf near Old Faithful, the rowdy campgrounds, people chattering on cell phones in the places that call for a cathedral-like silence, the runaway development in the gateway towns (my favorite, cynically speaking, being Grizzly Village, the theme park in West Yellowstone that advertises the complete "Yellowstone experience" a hundred yards from the west entrance). These can all be ignored if you make some effort, but it's easy to let them overwhelm you.

One of the few convincing lessons life has taught me is that cynicism, while bracingly astringent in small doses, doesn't lead very far, not in literature, not in philosophy, not on vacation. It's a sterile attitude—and yet I'm a contemporary American novelist, which means I'm pretty good at it if I want to be, and driving through the park, keeping my eyes open, lots of mordant zingers have to be choked back, especially with no one else in the car with whom to share them.

(My kids, in a teenage kind of way, can be pretty cynical; my response to this is to always out-cynical them. Hey, you want to be cynical? Try *this* on for size! . . . and I always leave them appalled.)

So, on my explorations of those first few days, I tried not letting the rvs towing suvs towing boat trailers get to me, just like I tried not letting the bison, so placid looking in repose, get a window of opportunity on my rear end. The problem with irony and cynicism is that I've never indulged myself in them deeply enough to find positive delight in the experience, à la H. L. Mencken—and now I suspect it's too late in life for that. Starting here in Yellowstone near my birthday, I'd better learn to temper the irony with some bemusement rather than letting it fester.

One of my finest days that first week began with a hike up Cascade Creek, just west of Canyon. There were no cars parked at the trailhead. I brought my bear spray along and fastened bear bells to my rucksack where they would jingle, hopefully in a key the bears found repellent. *Don't hike alone!* rangers tell you, and if you do, *make noise.* The bells, to my ear, were a bit too mellow, so I attempted to make myself more discordantly obnoxious by banging my rod case on the rocks and singing the first thing that popped into my throat, which happened to be Manchester United's soccer fight song, sung to the tune of "The Battle Hymn of the Republic": "Glory, glory, Man Uniiii . . . ted!"

It worked—I saw no grizzlies. A mile into the woods, I detoured over to the stream, Cascade Creek, which is set in a beautiful meadow with a view toward Mount Washburn. These Yellowstone meadows are as sweet and secret places as you can imagine, especially in autumn, when the willows and alders turn golden and you're guaranteed to have things to yourself. These resemble alpine meadows in their openness, in the way the grass waves in the wind, but they also tend to be surprisingly boggy, so there's the kind of mystery that comes with being in a swamp. Cascade Creek cuts through the center of this in serpentine meanderings that allow you to take shortcuts over the sandy isthmuses and sneak up on the trout from different angles.

Under drought conditions, the little cutthroats were very wary—much harder to fool than the brookies back in Blacktail Deer Creek. I went down to 7X on my leader, which is to say that I was fishing for them on sheerest gossamer, but anything heavier on the water would send them fleeing upstream in a tizzy.

But that was all right—this was my day of *not* fishing seriously, and what I did most of the morning was lie against a log in the center of the meadow enjoying the scenery, not thinking about anything profound, mostly staring. Or at least I tried doing this. Various concerns intruded before I could relax completely. One concern was the possible proximity of grizzlies; traveling alone in the backcountry, you can't shake this feeling entirely—and it's not necessarily a bad feeling either. Concern number two was that maybe the trout were bigger and dumber a half mile upstream and I should be up there fishing. Concern number three was the ordinary background worry that, when you're my age, with a family, never goes completely away, even in Yellowstone.

After a while the tug-of-war grew fierce—the brilliant immediacy of my surroundings versus all this worrisome, hateful buzz. I felt mad that I couldn't relax completely—and when you get mad at not relaxing, the game is up. I went back to fishing, since its concentration is all about immediacy, living in the moment, sharing the same spontaneous time line as the trout. But shouldn't I be able to achieve that just sitting on my butt?

I had a companion, I realized then. There under the pine tree that grew farthest out in the meadow—a buffalo bull, all by his lonesome, brown and stocky and perfectly content, gravely munching on something he found in the little slough where the swampy part began, aware of me, but totally indifferent.

I read later that an older male can eventually become a nuisance to the herd, attacking young ones with no provocation, to the point where the stronger, younger males drive him out, banishing him to exile. I was to see a good many lone buffalo during my three weeks; they always seemed waiting at the farthermost point of my fishing and hiking expeditions, so I began to believe it was the same buffalo that was following me around the park. This made for a strong fellow feeling, though I had actively sought my exile, not been banished. (Well, not exactly; I'd been grumpy all year, and I don't think anyone at home was sorry to see me temporarily go.)

My intention was to stay on the creek all afternoon, but my restlessness made this difficult. I got to thinking about the grizzlies again, remembered my promise to call home before the kids went to bed, worried over the construction delays I could expect heading back to Mammoth, remembered, totally out of the blue, an embarrassing junior high school dance I attended in 1962 . . . well, the list hardly matters. I put it down to illustrate the wretched background worry that makes it hard for me to sit in an unspoiled meadow letting the beauty of it soak in.

As much as I valued my time alone in the backcountry, I always enjoyed running into someone when I emerged from the woods. On this first hike, when I came again to the trailhead, a large stock trailer was spinning up dust as a pickup, its delivery accomplished, pulled it back onto the road. Where the dust settled, cinching the pack on the lighter colored of two lively looking horses, was a park ranger dressed in green firefighter pants and a white, v-necked t-shirt.

We talked. He was on his way into the wild country past Grebe Lake for the start of a two-week patrol. He was young, certainly no more than thirty, and with his slightly odd garb, his glass lenses which were purple-shaded on top like a mafia don's, he looked like the kind of man who goes his own way in life, certainly in small things, perhaps in big. We ended up talking for a good half hour. I was impressed with his packhorse (it was the rifle scabbard slanting downward that got to me); he, I imagined, was glad to take this last opportunity to chat with anyone for a lonesome fortnight.

I asked about poaching. Yes, it was still a problem in the park, he said. Just last year they had busted a not-very-intelligent ring of elk poachers who, to attract clients, went around to hunting and fishing shows in the winter, showing videos of their successful hunts—videos that were obviously taken in Yellowstone. I asked about bears. No, they didn't worry the horses particularly, and if one of them shied or snorted, it was almost always on account of a mountain lion, not a grizz.

To say that I envied him, riding off literally into the sunset, all his earthly possessions (well, the possessions that count) strapped to his packhorse, is an understatement. We were having a fine talk in the way men do, and I was just deciding that he valued me as his equal when he very gently punctured my bubble.

"Can I see your fishing permit, sir?"

Well, no harm done—he was working, after all. I wished him well as he rode off, turning in his saddle to make sure the packhorse followed. For a moment I wished I was him, another person—and that's not something I wish very often.

That night, in an odd mood, I tried an experiment that needs a bit of explanation.

There inevitably comes a point in a certain kind of novel written for women of a certain age where the heroine slowly strips before a full-length mirror, shy before her own nakedness, finally getting up the nerve to confront her own reflection. Her face? Not bad, she decides—though where did that new, shadowy line come from, the one curling down from the corner of her mouth like an italicized comma? Her breasts? Still firm, hardly any sag worth mentioning. Her tummy? Well, three childbirths had left their mark, but the years of sit-ups and aerobics had kept things even.

Men in novels don't stare into mirrors much, at least not heroes in their fifties. Middle-age men in locker rooms, it's been my experience, don't stare into mirrors much either, and when they do it's just to give a couple of nostalgic brush swipes to what's left of their hair. But maybe, for me, a middle-aged man who has come to Yellowstone National Park to confront the state of his body, mind and soul, a little more of this wouldn't hurt: staring into a mirror, turning on the x-ray machine, inserting myself into my own personalized, do-it-yourself CAT scanner, doing inventory, seeing how things stand. The state of the body, its always difficult relationship with the mind, how it's doing and not doing under what's starting to be the weight of some fairly significant mileage: this was perforce occupying more and more of my time anyway, there was no use in being shy.

So. Off with the fishing shirt, the black fleece pants, the high-tech underwear—it's time a man was given the chance to strip in print. There. Naked. Honest. No excuses.

The first test is a tough one. Many people, after not looking at themselves this closely for many years, would immediately throw their hands across their faces in horror, so different are their silhouettes from what they were in their prime. And yes, I do feel a certain shock and surprise, but only because the body I see in the mirror is so much more svelte and fit than the one I spent a troubled youth with. Those were my days of a quart of milk at dinnertime, followed by half an apple pie; my days of having a forty-four-inch waist; the days when my mother took me to the "Husky" section of Grant's when it came time to buy pants. I paid for this in a lot of ways, physical and social, but the nice thing about an overweight adolescence (the traces of which remain in indelible purple-pink stretch marks along my flanks) is that I can enjoy the rare pleasure of feeling a whole lot better about my body shape at fifty-five than I did at eighteen.

That's overall, the vital first impression. Staring closer, I decided to start at the brain, not only what I can see of it on the surface, but what my inner scan told me must surely be going on underneath. My head is massive—never have I met anyone with a bigger hat size—and it is clear that this is one part of the body that will maintain the same dimension regardless of the shrinkages and expansions elsewhere.

My forehead is still tight, firm and relatively unblemished. Acne had learned along time ago that things were too hot up there, too much friction and buzz to find it a suitable place for habitation. Behind the forehead? Inner brain? Well, I am getting a *little* forgetful when it comes to short-term memory—nothing serious, perfectly natural . . . or is it? This has been a fairly recent development in the history of being late-middle-aged, and it isn't pleasant. A name I know perfectly well but which won't quite come; a silly mix-up over a date I should have remembered; calling my daughter by my son's name. Harmless, or at least it used to be, only now neurologists have taught us that this can be the most dangerous and horrendous warning the brain is capable of delivering. Even if there were do-it-yourself brain scanners capable of checking on the current trends of the inner brain, something that could predict the future, most people my age wouldn't have the guts to switch it on.

My hair, on the other hand, presented me with largely positive news, thanks be to genetics. My grandfather boasted a fine shock of white hair all the way into his nineties; my father, age eighty-seven, still visited the barber regularly. What's different in my own case is the color. I'm a redhead—perhaps among the country's oldest living redheads whose hair is still certifiably red. It's browner and duller than it was when I was young, but there is still a lot more color there (autumn color) than any other fifty-year-old I've ever run into, especially all those bald guys nicknamed "Red."

Red hair has always been both my pride and my vulnerability, very similar in this respect to Cyrano de Bergerac's famous nose. It prompted much teasing when I was little, helped make me shy. At six, when every adult you meet immediately gushes, "Where on earth did you get that gorgeous red hair?" or every kid nags, "Hey carrot-top!", you tend to retreat into a shell. (Driven deeper in by adults, female adults, who, apprised of your name, immediately started singing, "Walter, Walter, lead me to the altar!") But—the good side—red hair always made me feel I was different, special, destined for a future out of the norm.

So—still a redhead after all these years. Some white is mixed in now—I'm not so vain as to deny the evidence. Salt and cayenne, that's what it looks like, and how much longer the authentically red strands will linger is anyone's guess. An even bigger mystery is what it will do to my self-esteem when, instead of marking me as different, my whitened hair blends me in with everyone else my age. Cyrano without the nose, without the panache, is a pitiful figure.

Anything else while we're up high like this? Ears? Pretty sharp yet (PRETTY SHARP YET!), though who knows how much longer this will last. Eyes? They're on the list of things needing checking, that endless list they toss at you once you turn fifty. My teeth are costing me a fortune, since boomers came along before fluoride was common and so inevitably our mouths are full of metal that now needs "restoration"; baby boomers, whatever else we're famous for, will go down in history as the last generation of Americans who suffered yellow teeth.

In even the most injury-prone body, the most heavily used and battered, there is usually at least one neutral ground, an organ, joint or limb that has behaved itself perfectly over the years, not caused any grief. You come to take it for granted, and that's a wonderful thing, to be able to ignore all those scare stories you hear on the news or read about in doctors' waiting rooms, warnings that get everyone else nervous, but to which—so high is your confidence in this one particular organ—you can remain blithely indifferent.

For me this safety zone, this bodily Switzerland, has always been my chest, lungs and heart. A decent amount of exercise has kept my wind strong; I've never smoked a single cigarette; modern advances in medicine, at least in developed countries, have all but eliminated the scourge of tuberculosis, which had always been the writers' way to die (Thoreau, Chekhov, Orwell—all my favorites). My heart hasn't been nearly as big a concern for me as it was to members of my father's generation, who, when they weren't worried about ulcers, fretted about coronaries, arrhythmia, angina.

Then, too, all the news you read on the heart seems to be good news, from the miracle cures of high-tech surgery, to the efficacy of tried-and-true remedies that have been here all along. Who cannot be cheered, for instance, by learning that a baby aspirin, taken once a day, can do wonders for the life span? Not just any aspirin—*baby* aspirin, what our mothers gave us when we were teething. Fatalists, though, would tell you that's exactly the part of the body you should fear most—the one that's always been well-behaved.

If my chest is my Switzerland, my tranquil Shangri-La, then the flip side, my back, is my Kosovo, my Haiti, my tumultuous

Middle East. All my body's drama and melodrama take place there; it is the smelter where the tension of daily living is converted into red-hot pain. And, looking hard into the mirror, it's easy to see why. Those round shoulders, that long torso, the torque between them all wrong, so the inward-pressing skeleton finds the discs at the base of the spine, squeezes them, and makes them yell. Apes, when they learned to walk erect, had not done me any genetic favors. I long ago gave up going to doctors about this, since not only are they of little help when it comes to your back, but they have a tendency to blame you for it. You lifted wrong, sat wrong, slept on the wrong mattress . . . all of which may be true, but there's something about the nagging, accusatory tone they use that only drives the pain deeper.

Turning around, moving over to where the light is stronger, I begin to examine my stomach. Having suffered that "husky" adolescence, having determined that for what I wanted to do in life I needed to be fit, needed to feel good about myself (the boomer motto), I have exercised a pretty ruthless self-control over the years as to what I've eaten—and the results have showed. At thirty, I realized that my metabolism was slowing down, and that I would have to adjust my eating habits accordingly. At forty, my eating habits prudently established, I unaccountably began gaining weight, and so had to calibrate again, to readjust. At fifty, damn if it didn't happen again—the metabolism slowing, the pounds arriving from nowhere, so yet again I'd had to cut back.

A flat tummy! So much self-discipline! So much self-denial! So much Puritan weighing of consequences, all those little moments of pride in a second helping refused, or guilt over a minor piece of cake.

You can judge a lot from a mirror, but of course not all. The inner stuff, organs—how strange it is to depend on them for everything, and yet to never be able to see them. It's like living on a lucrative pension from a distant relative you've not once met in person, or, if things go wrong, like being punished by an evil dictator whose face you've never even seen on TV. We take it on faith that our kidneys, our livers, our pancreases are really there, but most people would have trouble pointing to where exactly in the body they are located. The *alleged* kidney, the *supposed* liver—that's what we make of them, we take them entirely on trust. What a strange kind of intimacy this creates—this symbiotic dance with an invisible partner, this blind, mysterious codependency.

But like so much else in the world, all this is changing. People can see inside themselves now: anyone, *you*, if you're crossing the 50 barrier and your primary-care physician tells you it's time for your first colonoscopy (a late-middle-age rite of passage now, the boomer bar mitzvah). It's a bizarre experience, sort of an exploratory trip, something like you might see on a *National Geographic* special about caves, and yet what is being explored are your vitals, your innards, and what might be discovered there isn't bats or a new kind of cave fish, but something that will mean the end for you, or at least a very serious change in how your life is conducted. This part of me is *real*, I remember thinking—it was the same reaction I got when I traveled to a destination I had read about all my life—and it was in the absolute surprise and marvel of this, with the doctor's lulling voice reassuring me at every fresh, encouraging centimeter of smooth inner flesh, that the anesthesia finally overcame me and I fell asleep.

The lower body is mostly a boring matter of mechanics at this stage, what's working, what's rusty, how the torque holds up in one joint, how the levers or pads are doing in another. Arthritis becomes a concern, which is the name given to those twinges and pains you can't otherwise account for. Cartilage is thinning everywhere, becoming less elastic, less cushioning. We're told to worry about our bones, wistfully recall our mothers urging us to drink more milk. The arch in our feet flattens; we make our first visits to a podiatrist, wait in a seedy waiting room with old people who, like members of a welcoming club, squeeze together on the couch to make room for you. Instead of skipping over the articles on artificial joint replacement, you now read them carefully, pray the technology improves as fast as they claim it will. ("Growing old is like being increasingly penalized for a crime you haven't committed," a British novelist once wrote, and he must have been referring to the joints.)

The man in the mirror had never been one to jog or run. I've always favored swimming or bike riding, and so compared to most aging athletes my knees are still reasonably functional. What I've discovered, though, is that joints have a very long, patient, vengeful memory; they can bide their time for forty years before reminding you of some grievous harm they suffered when you were younger. I broke both elbows mountain climbing when I was twenty-four, and had no subsequent problem with them until now, when in reaching for something high, fly-fishing, even swimming, there come matching pains, one in the right elbow, one in the left, particularly nagging and hateful pains, revenge being so dark and sordid an emotion.

But there is good news, too. My fingers still fly lightly and quickly over a keyboard—a typewriter keyboard, since my Luddite reluctance to use a computer has spared me the trendy carpal tunnel problems suffered by so many of my peers. My legs are in good shape, too. "The legs go first," they say in sports, but my thighs are the strongest part of me, solid, pillar-like, supportive, the envy of the rest of my body, my best-behaved muscles.

As mentioned, it's not a natural thing for a man my age to stare into a mirror very long; perhaps it's time to be merciful and allow myself to turn away. But I've not been totally honest with my self-exam; there's one organ I've hardly touched upon, in many ways the most obvious and vital. If you are your own best judge when it comes to the various internal clocks, dials and gauges you carry around inside, it's quite different when it comes to the external part of you, the covering, your skin. When people decide whether someone looks young or old, what they're usually judging is how your skin looks. If your skin is taut, you're still young; if your skin is wrinkled, you're old—this is the cruel, unjust syllogism that governs things, and it doesn't leave someone my age much in the way of middle ground in which just to *be*.

Skin is both the façade we present to the outside world and our protection from it; it's the part of our body that not only carries the most metaphoric weight, but reflects most accurately the kind of life we've led. (And how oddly delicate and fragile skin is, even when young; as essayist Andrea Jones puts it, "There should be more than this flimsy dermal bubble separating the vastness of the cosmos from the throb of blood and consciousness that is you.") Everyone over forty is responsible for their own face, it has been said, but this also might be said of the skin. (The great essayist Montaigne reminds us that "old age plants more wrinkles in the mind than it does on the face.")

If contemporary fiction is any guide, then, at least for women, skin's first trouble spot is on the back of the elbow. In many novels, that's where the heroine first sees her flesh sag in a way that seems cruelly inexplicable. That pouch beginning to droop away from the bone, flesh pouting in boredom and fatigue, in the very part of the body you might think would remain eternally taut from all that flexing. This can be alarming to overly sensitive souls—never mind that this sagging usually starts when you're nine or ten.

For me, it was on my legs where I first noticed my skin changing in this way; this was brand-new, something that had just become visible in the weeks before my trip West. If I cross my legs, stare down at the relaxed flesh on the underside of my calf, I can see that the skin is very lightly wrinkled. And not just random wrinkles—chevrons in parallel lines that flow upward toward the bottom of my knees, like the tide running along a sandy beach, or rather, the kind of scalloped lines left when the water recedes.

I know what this is—it is aging made visible. And, for the time being anyway, it's a far from ugly phenomenon—it really *does* look like lines on a beach—though I can't see it without sensing an overwhelming poignancy, I who am so good at finding poignancy in others, but hardly ever in myself. What's more, I can find similar lines on my arms beneath my remaining freckles, though there it's more a delicate crosshatching, the kind you might see on an exquisitely drawn map. Again, these lines are aligned with each other in perfect symmetry. What I had never realized before was that my body had a natural grain to it, and that these wrinkles were aligning themselves with that grain as they formed; they knew something about my body, my essence, that I was just discovering myself.

I'm grainy—what a strange, unexpected discovery for a man my age to make. And how curiously out-of-body the realization is; I could have been staring at an exhibit in a science museum or at a sculpture at an art gallery. It was the late-middle-age moment in its purest form—a moment of surprise, shock, recognition, to discover that aging is a real phenomenon after all, and that it can best be described, not as being over the hill now, but as the tide starting to go out.

It was my habit every morning, after brewing up a cup of tea, to spread a Yellowstone map open on the bed or the little desk the cabin provided, and plot my route for the day. I'd begin by staring down at the map, giving me, as it were, a view from outer space, but eventually, hungry for detail, increasingly engaged, I'd bend down closer, pick the map up, lie on my back, and hold it at arm's length above my chest, so it was now an earthier view I had, similar, say, to a solitary old bison's staring up at the encircling ridges and peaks.

There were two maps I used. The first was the one everyone is handed when they enter the park, the Park Service's, with its scarlet delineation of roads, grayish shading for topography, splashes of blue for ponds and lakes—these, and a whole smorgasbord of little icons showing where the campgrounds are, the picnic tables, the lodging. For finer detail, I used a recreational map I'd bought in Bozeman fifteen years earlier—tattered, stained with ancient smears of bug juice and sunscreen, engraved with illegible notes written to myself on trips past, even smoky (it seemed) from the great fires; creased where it was never meant to be creased, it seemed one puff away from utter disintegration. So I was gentle with it—and yet its evocative depiction of the park's rivers, the way it delineated every little bend and curve, made it much more suggestive and useful than the other maps I found.

An anonymous master of cartography had created this map. Its hot springs seemed to sulfurously steam; its geysers were so real that I was afraid to put my face too close.

By now I was something of a connoisseur of Yellowstone maps. How many winter evenings I had spent daydreaming over this one and then that, plotting a way to fish three streams in the morning and two more in the afternoon, or tracing with my finger routes deep into the interior that I would almost certainly never hike. For me—and I suspect for many other lovers of the park—the Yellowstone map has become iconic over the years, a shape, a pattern that once depicted, even on a postcard or a souvenir scarf, is immediately recognizable—similar in this respect to the famous map of the London underground.

I'm looking down at the official map right now, taking the long view. The shape it depicts is almost perfectly square and straight-edged, at least on the south and west; its perimeter, the thick green line, is bold and dramatic, suggesting—even if you don't know its history—a government that for once did something imaginative with its power, squaring off a huge corner of the country and stamping it as special. And there's sensitivity apparent, too, or how else to explain that little wavy corner in the northeast, where the boundary curves and wiggles to include some petrified trees, or that deep inward curve in the east that tucks in and protects the westward-flowing tributaries of Yellowstone Lake. A fine, powerful something was responsible for creating this shape—that's the impression that first hits me looking at the map from afar—and the miracle of this underlines every detail and feature after zooming in.

There are other broad strokes beside the park's brave perimeter. The road system, the pattern it makes, hasn't changed much in a

hundred years, the current paved roads being modern updates of
the old carriage roads, which in turn followed old Indian trails or
the routes of the earliest explorers. They don't go *everywhere*—that's
the reassuring message the map's red lines first give you—with
the core formed by the Norris–Canyon–West Thumb–Madison
Junction loop, and five spokes branching off toward the park's
borders. Looking at the map, studying its superimpositions, the
red lines remind me of the outline of a skate, the kind you might
find washed up on a sandy beach, the carapace that squarish
central oval, with antennae branching off to the north, south, east
and west. (A Yellowstone map provides something of a Rorschach
test for those who study it closely.)

Along with the roads, there are two conspicuous lines drawn on
the map. One, a great circle enclosing the central carapace, is the
boundary of the ancient caldera, showing where, 600,000 years
ago, inconceivably large amounts of molten rock exploded toward
the surface, crested, then collapsed, leaving a huge encircling rim
roughly forty-five miles by thirty-five miles around and a half mile
deep—a rim that's a key to understanding the landscape as you
drive the park. The other line (amber-colored on the official map)
marks the Continental Divide, and unlike the caldera boundary,
it loops every which way, which is one of the reasons the early
explorers had so much trouble making sense of the watersheds.
Exploring Two Ocean Plateau in the park's remote southeast corner, Jim Bridger was as fascinated by this as by any feature in the
park: the possibility of a "Two Ocean River" starting out as one
stream high in the mountains, then spitting into a Pacific branch
emptying into the Snake River, and an Atlantic branch, flowing
toward the Missouri.

What's reassuring about staring at a Yellowstone map is knowing that for well over a century it hasn't changed by more than a wrinkle—the broad outline stamped on the landscape in 1872 still protects it. What was terrifying to those lovers of the park who studied newspaper maps during the great fires of '88 was how this boundary, this protective wall, was suddenly breached—and that the danger came from *within* those broad perimeter lines, not from without. These maps showed a new and hateful crosshatching that marked the outlines of the various fires, and each week these grew, until the map was almost entirely splotched with them, and very little was *not* crosshatched. There were the Clover and Mist fires in early July, little innocuous amoebas on the map in the northeast, but then in August they combined into one huge circle, the Clover-Mist fire now, matched by the Red-Shoshone fire to the southeast of Yellowstone Lake, the North Fork fire threatening Old Faithful, the Fan fire raging unchecked in the northeast, and the Mint Creek fire to the southeast. This is what the Yellowstone map had suddenly become, a montage of new and terrifying shapes christened with names of evil portent—and twenty years later the memory of this reminds me that the map I'm staring at is not of a static land protected beneath a glass dome, but a dynamic, ever-changing landscape that literally bubbles, shakes, heaves, and—once every couple of centuries—burns.

There is something else to keep in mind when you stare down at a Yellowstone map: how deeply into the American experience this space remained almost totally blank. The first map to resemble today's wasn't drawn until after the Washburn Expedition returned to Helena in 1870, and the first trained cartographer capable of bringing any precision to bear on the terrain, Anton Schoenborn, only came to the area in 1872 as a member of the Hayden survey party—1872 being the year the park was formally established.

Less than 150 years ago, then, this land was largely terra incognita, which, on my personal time scale, means until almost yesterday. The oak table I'm typing these words on, bought at a yard sale, is more than 150 years old; the thickest maples I can see out my study window were planted in the 1870s; in 1872, my grandfather's father was a full-grown man. Snap your fingers, blink your eyes, and this so-familiar, much-loved map dissolves, the land along the Upper Yellowstone becomes again what it was for so long: a land of rumor, fable and legend, with no one alive in the world, no one, with enough knowledge to sketch more than a hopeful outline of where these rumored wonders might lie.

Or consider this: this plateau had a name long before it was actually discovered. An anonymously drawn map of 1797, prepared for the early fur trappers, referred to a Missouri tributary as the "R. des Roches Jaunes," which may have referenced the yellow sandstone bluffs along the Yellowstone's lower reaches, or, more intriguingly, may have meant the yellowish lava of the future park's Grand Canyon. The name stuck—and right from those first years seemed drenched in an aura of uncertainty and legend. In 1805, as the first discoveries of the Lewis and Clark Expedition began filtering back east, General James Wilkinson, governor of the Louisiana Territory (and a notorious wannabe traitor), forwarded to Washington a letter summing up the latest Missouri River rumors, referring to "among other things a little incredible, a volcano distinctly described on Yellow Stone River."

It's too bad we can't honor the person, probably a Minnetaree Indian, who first gave the river—and the region around its headwaters—its name. A place name of genius, so inspired that much of the original magic and mystery clings to it still. There's that interesting contradiction right up front—stone isn't usually yellow, so the adjective surprises us and stands out—and then the further irony of the softness of the first two syllables working against the adamantine hardness of the third. Yellow suggests gold, and gold prospectors would quickly swarm in here, but it also suggests magic, so "Magic Stone" is how the mind takes the word in. And its beat is alluring, too; it's a word that said out loud or even read on the page carries with it its own impetuous rhythm. Yellowstone. *Yellowstone*. It's a word that suggests wonderland all on its own—and so it's no wonder that right from the moment of its original usage it became associated with something uniquely special and extraordinarily odd.

Reading at night about what historian Aubrey Haines aptly describes as the "extended drama" of Yellowstone discovery, I was struck by one anomaly. Throughout the entire history of American discovery, time and time again, people were far too credulous about what lay beyond the boundaries of the settled world. Cathy lay there, or the Seven Cities, or the Northwest Passage, or the magic Indian kingdom of Norumbega. Just one more expedition, one more push, and the magic will be captured, appropriated, tamed. Always the human imagination outraced the facts, wondrous as many of these facts were. With Yellowstone—and only with Yellowstone—the story is exactly the opposite. As the first reports began working their way eastward, people's imaginations couldn't believe things like geysers and hot springs and mud volcanoes actually existed. And by the 1860s the gullible had been burned so many times that they were turning skeptical, even cynical; people weren't about to be fooled again by extravagant wonders that turned out to be chimerical. At every step of the way in the American experience, the human imaginative capacity had inflated reality; with Yellowstone, the human imagination finally met its match. In time, this contradiction would add to the park's allure.

As Paul Schullery puts it (and, with Haines, he's one of the Yellowstone historians worth reading), "The initial reluctance of the world to believe the wild tales of Yellowstone's many wonders served only to heighten interest in the place when the truth was finally confirmed."

And so the "extended drama" took on a pattern right from the start. A small party of roughnecks stumbles upon the Yellowstone plateau during a search for riches, either in peltry or gold. One of the party turns out to be literate and writes a letter home to his family in the East, mentioning, almost casually, the wonders they had stumbled upon. The letter gets printed in an eastern newspaper, but is put down as just another of the trappers' tall tales. Another party penetrates the plateau, another account is brought back, and each time this happens a teasing increment of further detail begins to emerge, prompting slightly more organized expeditions . . . and yet, withal, the opaque Yellowstone curtain never fully lifts. The land was trapped out by the frighteningly early date of 1840; gold prospectors never found pay dirt; the Civil War shut exploration down for a vital five years; the original inhabitants, the placid Sheepeaters, only wanted to be left alone and didn't cause enough trouble for the authorities to bother exterminating them in organized campaigns.

Within this pattern, several things stand out. John Colter is given credit for being the first white man to see Yellowstone, on a solo winter journey in 1807, the only documentary evidence for which is a brief caption on William Clark's map of the West, on which is delineated, toward the headwaters of a vague Yellowstone River, a large "Lake Eustis," and, more intriguingly, an area of "Hot Spring Brimstone"—which established the hellish, otherworldly associations Yellowstone would not shed for many years. Trappers from the Canadian North West Company may have penetrated the area in 1818, encountering "boiling fountains." A trapper known only by the initials "J. O. R." carved these and the date "August 18, 1819," onto a tree near the Upper Falls, an etching that was discovered many years later—J. O. R. being the first tourist, but not the last, to immortalize himself in graffiti.

A new breed of literate trapper began with a Pennsylvanian named Daniel Potts. He was part of a large organized party on horseback, which, having evaded dangerous Blackfoot raiders, managed to reach the area of the future park in the summer of 1824. His letters home, published in the *Philadelphia Gazette and Daily Advertiser*, form the first published description of Yellowstone's wonders:

The Yellow-stone has a large freshwater Lake near its head on the very top of a Mountain which is about one hundred by forty miles in diameter and as clear as crystal on the south borders of this lake is [a] number of hot and boiling springs some of water and others of most beautiful fine clay and resembles that of a mush pot and throws its particles to the immense height of from twenty to thirty feet. . . . There is also a number of places where the pure sulphor is sent forth in abundance one of our men Visited one of those wilst taking his recreation there at an instant the earth began a tremendous trembling and he with difficulty made his escape.

An observant and curious clerk working for the American Fur Company, one Angus Ferris, was stimulated by all the rumors to deliberately visit the plateau in 1833, to see whether the reports of great geysers along the Firehole River were true—a visit that gave him, in Aubrey Haines's words, the "triple distinction of being the first tourist to visit the Yellowstone wonders; the first to provide an adequate description of a geyser, and the first to apply the word 'geyser' to Yellowstone thermal features." And a fourth distinction, too, it must be said: pressed for time, Ferris spent only several hours among the geysers, thereby establishing the hey-that's-beautiful-now-we're-out-of-here syndrome replicated by millions of visitors in the years since.

Osborne Russell, another tough-but-sensitive New Age trapper, came to the park area in 1835, and was probably the first Yellowstone writer who had enough adjectives to do the landscape justice. "There is something in the wild romantic scenery of this valley (the Lamar) which I cannot describe," he wrote. "The impressions made upon my mind while gazing from a high eminence on the surrounding landscape one evening as the sun was gently gliding behind the western mountains were such as time can never efface from my memory." And so on, in this rapturous, wholly unprecedented vein. But friend Osborne could be soberly evocative if he had to be; witness his pithy description of what would later be called the Grand Prismatic Spring. "From the west side for one third of the diameter it was white, in the middle it was pale red, and the remaining third on the east light sky blue." A nice summation, and it's too bad that Russell, with a couple of arrows in his thigh, was run out of Yellowstone by a party of Piegan Indians.

The famous scout Jim Bridger knew Yellowstone like he knew most of the Rocky Mountain West, but his reputation for telling tall tales made people shrug off his stories of what could be seen there. Gold prospectors, famous for exaggerating what they wanted exaggerated and keeping mum about what they wanted to keep secret, weren't the most credible witnesses either, though these became the men who next brought back intriguing dribbles of more detail: Walter De Lacy, Charles Ream, John C. David, Bart Henderson, George Huston. The latter led a party into the Firehole in the autumn of 1864, but his party was so frightened by the geysers that they apparently bolted right back out again. "Their experience in late fall," Haines writes, "when the cold air was vapor-laden and thought by them to be suffocatingly obnoxious, developed a persistent myth of 'death valley,' which did nothing to encourage further visits." Still, the essential details of Yellowstone were largely known by 1870 — only known in a scattered, disorganized way, in the experience of illiterate trappers and close-mouthed miners, with no one interested enough or educated enough to weave the rumors and fragments into one compelling narrative rich enough in specific detail to be believed.

Deliberate attempts to construct this narrative, put the pieces together, draw a map, began with an expedition sent out in 1856 by Lieutenant Gouverneur Warren (whose heroics would one day save the Union at Gettysburg), followed by another expedition led by Capt. William F. Raynolds in 1860. Both forays were total failures, with Raynolds, attempting to force his party into Yellowstone through the steep mountain barrier to the southeast, not even making it into the future park at all.

A trio of amateurs pulled off the first successful expedition designed specifically to seek out Yellowstone's wonders. The Civil War had ended, and the floodgates of energy, ambition, gumption and greed had opened upon Montana in full strength. Two men employed by the Boulder Ditch Company, accompanied by a friend, decided to make a hunting, exploring trip to the Yellowstone area in the autumn of 1869 (how many of these explorations seemed, like mine, to take place in autumn), even though other would-be companions dropped out through fear of Indians.

The Folsom-Cook-Peterson expedition was the first recogniz-
ably modern Yellowstone journey, in that they saw most of the
marvels and marveled appropriately. They measured the Upper
and Lower Falls with a ball of twine and a rock, and, at least with
the former, came very close to the true figure of 109 feet; when
they came to the Great Fountain Geyser at sunset, just as it began
to play, they spontaneously took off their hats and yelled. Made
uneasy by those hellish early reports, they moved through the
Upper Geyser Basin very gingerly. "Although we experienced no
bad effects from passing through the Valley of Death," Folsom
explained, "yet we were not disposed to dispute the propriety of
giving it that name."

Their journey would have made more of an impact were it not
for Folsom's worry that if they told the truth about what they had
seen they would be branded as hopeless liars — not an epithet an
up- and-coming young man would have wanted attached to his
name. When asked to give a lecture in Helena, Folsom declined,
because "he was unwilling to risk his reputation for veracity by
a full recital, in the presence of strangers, of the wonders he had
seen."

Smart man, David Folsom. He understood perfectly the key
point—that the human imagination, even as late as 1869, was not
quite equal to the truth. He did, however, talk about the discoveries to several prominent Helena citizens, whetting their curiosity
to the point that they determined to visit the Yellowstone region
the following autumn, thereby setting the stage for the famous
Washburn Expedition, about which I was reading each night when
I came back tired and happy from my own latter-day explorations.
(And the fact that Yellowstone is so little changed today from 1870
makes reading about its history a much less abstract experience

than, say, reading about early New York City.) The Washburn
Expedition turned out to be the key moment in the long, catch-
up battle the truth had with myth—and what happened during
that magic autumn of 1870, Washburn's travels and travails, is
something I'll need to return to a bit further on.

One of the most surprising discoveries of my first week in the
park was that Yellowstone is inhabited by ghosts. Friendly ghosts,
shades of my own happy memories, and yet haunting and intimi-
dating even so.

That morning I'd gone back to fish the Soda Butte in the Lamar
Valley. Like a lot of people who love the park, this is my favorite corner, with its wide and exhilarating expanse, its mountain
encirclement, its surprising solitude. There are no spectacular
waterfalls along the Lamar, no splashy geysers, and, with the
road to Cooke City being something of a dead-end, it doesn't
get anywhere near the number of drive-through tourists that the
rest of the park sees. Add to that the elk and wolf spotting, the
excellent fishing, and I badly needed to spend another day there
before moving on.

It's funny, traveling alone. When you're with someone else,
even someone who pretty much thinks alike, the day and what
to do with it becomes a matter of delicate negotiation and com-
promise. You tentatively float an idea . . . your companion takes
it in, suggests a slight variation, or elaboration . . . you mention
something you've really been wanting to do, which they agree
with, especially since that would mean time to do something
they've really been wanting to do . . . and so on, until the day, like
the Treaty of Versailles, is diplomatically thrashed out.

When you're by yourself, much the same thing goes on, and yet the person across the negotiation table is yourself, the timid part of you that must be coaxed into trying something more adventurous, and the bolder, imprudent side, who must occasionally be tamed. Since *anything* is possible, the choices can be a bit overwhelming, and there is nothing stopping you from changing your mind. If you're something of a Libra when it comes to changing your mind anyway, this can mean an awful lot of switched intentions in the course of a routine day.

Plan A was to walk up to Trout Lake. This is a gem of a mountain tarn, reached by a short hike up a wildflower-dotted slope, and, small as it is, the cutthroat trout grow larger than they do anywhere else in the park. (On my last visit there, three years previously, I'd come upon an eight-pound trout, bronzed and blackened with age, gasping out its life in the shallows.) I parked at the small, inconspicuous trail sign, strung up my rod, stuffed some blueberry scones left over from breakfast into my day pack, strapped the bear spray to my hip, went through my fly box looking for winners . . . got ready, got set, but didn't quite go.

The problem was that trail sign, the one fashioned of a cedar post and a little wood-burned crosspiece reading *Trout Lake .6 mi.* There's a picture of me taken in 1995 that's been hanging in my office ever since that involves that sign and a memorable family vacation. We, all four of us, had just gotten back from a hike to Trout Lake, a morning filled with laughter and melodrama and high excitement, as Erin, Matthew and Celeste pointed to cruising trout which Dad, to everyone's amazement, actually succeeded in catching. Hiking back down to the car, Celeste had the three of us pose up against the sign—and the result is one of the best, most cherished photos of the hundreds we have.

I'm in my fishing duds, tall enough that my elbow rests on

the sign with my fly rod pointed sideways out of the frame; even wearing sunglasses, it's obvious that my face is wreathed in happiness and pride. Far below, a whole generation below, hugging the sign's pole with one arm, hugging my silver fly rod case with the other, is Matthew, age five; he's got a blue- and-black striped shirt on, baggy sweatpants, a hat that is even floppier and more ridiculous than anything I wear myself, and, under his glasses, a smile that is simply irresistible. Erin stands shoulders and head above him to his right; she's got purple tights on which match the purple laces of her hiking boots, a white sweatshirt and blue hat; hanging from her shoulder is our canteen, and wrapped around the strap is a bandanna the same purple color as almost everything else; her smile is just as happy as Matt's, if a bit more secret and self-contained.

It's the picture I was remembering as I got ready to hike . . . and it was too much for me; that nagging case of homesickness that had been latent all trip came back again, only this time with redoubled power and force. Hike up to where we had had one of our best family adventures ever? Hike up there alone to brood? No, I don't think so, not today. Trout Lake's happy ghosts would not be stirred.

Time for Plan B. A few miles to the west is the dirt road that leads up to Slough Creek campground. Slough Creek, the northern tributary of the Lamar that flows down from some of the park's finest mountains, is a place most visitors never learn about, though to fly-fishers it has a legendary reputation. When someone says, "I've been fishing Slough," you're supposed to ask, "Second Meadow or First?" First is an hour's hike up a fairly steep trail, and it has some of the largest, wariest cutthroat in the park; Second is an hour further, a destination for hotshots, with trout that are just as big as in First Meadow, but somewhat easier to fool.

I'd fished them both over the years with my partner Ray Chapin; on one memorable trip to Second, we'd fled into a copse of trees to avoid a thunderstorm, only to end up in the den of some wild animal, littered with half-munched bones. ("Grizz," Ray confidently opined; "they wait for thunderstorms to chase fishermen in here, then they pounce.") We'd gotten a little tired of the long hikes, the numbers of fly-fishers encountered at the end, so we had pioneered a stretch below the campground we took to calling "Minus One Meadow," which, if you're someone who knows the river, means about a half a mile upstream of the famous "v.i.p." pool.

It's lovely water, with a slow, tricky current that carries pale morning duns and other mayflies down to incredibly snobby and sophisticated trout, who cruise the shallows, turning up their noses even at real flies if they don't float quite the way they favor. The fishing is demanding, but we'd done well there, and the hike in from the road is just long enough to keep it relatively secret.

I parked in the little pullout where you leave your car, strung up my rod again, checked to make sure the scones were still in my backpack, that I had plenty of sunscreen and water . . . started up that first steep sage-covered hill . . . went twenty yards . . . and came to a halt. Did I really want to fish there alone, without Ray who was as much a part of the experience as the Slough Creek water itself? Of course I did. I walked thirty yards more, got to the top of the hill and the first wide view of the meadow in the distance. Did I want to fish it alone, without having Ray to call to for suggestions for flies, without seeing him race off downstream attached to an enormous trout only he could ever catch up with, without having him sitting on the bank above me, casting some shade, as we took a break for lunch? Sure I did . . . didn't I?

I won't embarrass myself my recounting how many times I started out for the river, stared, remembered, hesitated, went on again, stopped, reconsidered. There was a sentimental barrier I could not penetrate—and so, after about a half mile of these comic starts and stops, I went back to the car, broke my rod down, ate a scone, and began casting around for Plan C.

I drove westward toward the Tower Junction bridge, then, just before crossing the Yellowstone, pulled over and parked. There is no official trail here, but it's relatively easy to climb a slight rise and follow the river's high bank downstream. This is the "Black Canyon," a tumultuous stretch of river where the surrounding walls, sheer and barren, make the water seem to rush all the faster—a vertiginous, dangerous stretch that even dedicated fishermen usually avoid. Ray and I had once followed this same path a half mile down to where the Lamar joins with the big river, and done exceptionally well, with cutthroat moving into the junction pool to get some relief from the heavy current, and, while they were at it, feasting on the swallow-sized salmon flies that blew into the Lamar's canyon from the Yellowstone's.

A happy memory, perhaps best not disturbed—but this was getting silly now, and I marched ahead with my plan. On that first trip I had spotted something I badly wanted to see again, an arrangement of rocks flowing down the canyon's side that seemed a bit too studied and arranged to be an accidental upheaval or the play of geologic chance. It was only my New Englander's eye, accustomed to spotting old stone walls or the foundations of long-vanished mills that even managed to identify it at all. "That's a bridge," I told Ray. "Or what's left of it." We walked over to the bank and peered down, but there was no sign, no historical marker, and it seemed incredible that anyone would have ever tried to build a bridge over the torrent we saw below.

I made it a point to learn more about these remains. In 1871 a remarkable prospector and scout named Jack Baronett, "Yellowstone Jack," wanting to profit from the gold discoveries on the Clarks Fork northeast of the future park, built a bridge over the Yellowstone near its junction with the Lamar—a ninety-foot-long stringer bridge of two spans, with a rock-filled pier erected on a handy shelf of bedrock. It was only by working in winter when the water was low that construction was possible; there was no other bridgeable spot for many miles upstream or down. Yellowstone Jack, with that bold piece of entrepreneurship, locked into a good thing; he collected tolls, not only from gold miners, but from the first tourists flocking into the otherwise bridgeless park. The Nez Perce, on their flight through the park in 1877 ahead of General O. O. Howard's pursuing troops, burned the stringers of the bridge's east abutment, but it was rebuilt in 1878, this time with trusses capable of supporting a wagon's weight, not just a packhorse's. Baronett's Bridge was a vital spot in the park's early history, mentioned in all the memoirs and journals of the period—which makes even more poignant its survival as a failed attempt at privatization and a barely recognizable slide of rocks.

The modern bridge at Tower junction crosses the Yellowstone with brash efficiency, but no charm whatsoever, and I felt better the moment it was out of sight. As mentioned, there is no signage for the Baronett ruins, few fishers bother with the hike, and so the path I followed along the canyon's high rim was one left by those super-efficient trail blazers, bison and elk. Their droppings were everywhere, dried mostly—this is the great northern winter range, and so most of this was January scat, having worked its way down through the snow until sometime during the May thaw it finally reached earth.

Not for the first time, it occurred to me that one of the great, unsung wonders of Yellowstone is the amazing amount of animal dung to be found in and around the sagebrush or underneath the pines. Once upon a prehistoric time, this must have been part of people's everyday experience, this absorbing engagement with the leavings of animals hunted or feared or both. It's easy to picture primitive humans tiptoeing around the great steaming mounds much as I did, studying intently their freshness or gathering it for fuel if it was dry. Yellowstone is one of the last places left in this country where you can still experience this vestigial kind of engagement with wild poop—an uncelebrated part of the Yellowstone experience that deserves at least one paragraph of tribute.

It didn't take long to reach the ruins of the bridge. If anything, they stood out more obviously than they had in summer, with the underbrush dying back now. The drought had significantly lowered the Yellowstone from the level it had been the last time I was there, and let me understand that, yes, with boldness, building a bridge here would indeed have been possible. There is no signage to mark the spot, no explanatory kiosk with multimedia displays, and to me that was one of the great satisfactions of being there—to be able to see the bittersweet workings of time without any distractions. Yellowstone's archaeological treasures, until recently, were largely ignored, though knowledgeable rangers have always known the whereabouts of old Sheepeater wickiups (conical structures of dried poles), hidden away in secret valleys, and old trapper cabins built by poachers when the park was in its infancy.

I found a smooth, suitably inclined scoop in the canyon's rim, sat down, and ate my lunch while I stared at what was left of Yellowstone Jack's old bridge. He was a remarkable man, all accounts suggested. A Scots immigrant, his resume included prospecting for gold in three continents, sailing on a trading vessel to China, serving as mate on a whaler in the Arctic, and, after a spell in the Confederate cavalry, working as a soldier of fortune under Maximilian in Mexico, followed by years of scouting in the American West. His name pops up everywhere in accounts of Yellowstone's early days—he wasn't called "Yellowstone Jack" for nothing. It was Jack who found Truman Evarts after his infamous thirty-seven days of being lost; Jack who served as a scout with the troops chasing Chief Joseph and the Nez Perce through the park. It's easy to imagine his feelings when, hot on their trail toward the Lamar, he came across the fire they had set on his bridge to retard pursuit.

Undaunted, Yellowstone Jack rebuilt his bridge, and had the satisfaction in the early autumn of 1883 of being President Chester A. Arthur's personal guide through the park, in a party that included Robert Todd Lincoln and General Philip Sheridan. Still later, Baronett would be one of the park's first assistant superintendents, and would still be spry enough in 1886 to act as a backcountry scout for the army when it took over Yellowstone's administration and cracked down on its notorious poachers. The government took away his bridge in 1894, and with the miserly $5,000 in compensation Jack outfitted a prospecting expedition to Alaska that ended in failure. In 1901 he was listed as an "indigent" living in Tacoma, owning only the memories attached to his famous nickname. His bridge died about the same time, abandoned in 1903 when a new concrete bridge was built upstream.

I sat for a long while, enjoying the way that time was all jumbled-up there, the complicated paradoxes that the remains suggested. The canyon rim, so high for the first half mile downstream from the road, dipped and softened just beyond where I was sitting, and looking carefully I could just make out the terraces cut into the bank where the wagon road climbed from the bridge. This impressed me even more than the fact that Baronett and his crew had managed to span the river. How on earth had the steep bank been climbed? I suppose these terraces were the answer, that packhorses or wagons had zigzagged their way carefully back and forth until they reached the plateau.

The wind came up while I sat there, and dampened the sound of the river, but it was still impressive. In a lifetime of sitting beside rivers, listening, I'm not sure I ever heard one make quite the sound the Yellowstone makes in Black Canyon. There are no splashy drumbeats, no rocky tremolos, only a low, bass-like whoosh-ing, as if the river is rushing too fast and too purposely to bother emitting fancy aural variations. A chilling sound, if you listen to it alone. I was glad to have the ruined bridge for company.

Jack Baronett had a cabin just to the west of his bridge; it was comfortable enough that President Arthur and General Sheridan rested there for several days on their tour of 1883, both notables at this stage experiencing the ill health that would soon take them. I found it very easy to picture what the scene must have been like, and all but impossible; the scenery was exactly that which had comforted them, but with no signs of people it was impossible to think that this had ever been a busy place, the center—at least for a few days—of the entire U.S. power structure. (I have to admit a sneaking fondness for Chester A. Arthur, a feeling I've had ever since I found we shared the same October birthday.)

This is one of the central paradoxes of the Yellowstone experience, and to describe it I have to risk not making any sense. Yellowstone seems the oldest place in America simply because it's *not* old; the landscape is so unchanged, so virgin, that I could sense the past there more strongly than I could, say, at Salisbury Cathedral or the Roman remains in Bath. Yellowstone is simultaneously the oldest place in America, since you see the past as *now*, and the youngest place in America, since magically it shrugs the centuries off, creation is still working right in front of you as it's worked there forever. Remembrance of things past is easy here because the backdrop is still present, imagination doesn't have to work too hard to summon back the feel of it all. This, at least to me, is exhilarating. You don't have to bother with nostalgia here; you don't have to be sad about time's corrosive touch. A lot of things drop away from you on a good Yellowstone visit, including, as I stared down at Baronett's ruined bridge in that burnished autumn sunlight, the tragic weight of years.

Do the ghosts of Chief Joseph, President Arthur and General Sheridan cross the bridge at night when no one is looking? I like to think they do. But with the sun getting lower in the sky now, the river making that lonely whooshing, I decided not to stick around to watch.

I drove the familiar Yellowstone loop road counterclockwise half-circle the next day, from Mammoth to Tower to Canyon to Lake. The name "Canyon" refers to the Grand Canyon of the Yellowstone, and when I came to the junction I drove over to take a look. "Approaching Inspiration Point," read the sign, and that was good for a smile—at last, a road sign meant just for me! There were only a handful of cars in the parking lot. Inspiration Point is out on a little boardwalk, and older couples were taking photos of each other with the falls as backdrop.

I'd seen the Lower Falls before, but never in autumn, and the shadows gave a steely texture to the dropping water, made the huge upsurge of spray seem molten. The sun was high enough that it turned the canyon canary yellow; as usual, it was a *long* way down.

Waterfalls are meant to induce solemn thoughts. Here is Nathaniel Pitt Langford's description of his own reaction as he viewed the scene in 1870, while a member of the Washburn Expedition; he was probably one of the first hundred white men to ever see the falls, and probably the first whose education gave him a Romantic frame of reference.

[The rapids] were so terrible to behold, that none of our company could venture the experiment in any other manner than by lying prone upon the rock, to gaze into its awful depths; depths so amazing that the sound of the rapids could not be heard. The stillness is horrible, and the solitary grandeur of the scene surpasses conception. You feel the absence of sound—the oppression of absolute silence. Down, down, down, you see the river attenuated to a thread. If you could only hear that gurgling river, lashing with puny strength the massive walls that imprison it and hold it in their dismal shadow, if you could but see a living thing in the depth beneath you, if a bird would but fly past you, if the wind would move any object in that awful chasm, to break for a moment the solemn silence which reigns there, it would relieve the tension of the nerves which the scene has excited, and with a grateful heart you would thank God that he had permitted you to gaze unharmed upon the majestic depths of his handwork. But as it is, the spirit of man sympathizes with the deep gloom of the scene, and the brain reels as you gaze into the profound and solemn solitude.

What a strange, overpowering, existential kind of reaction (and I don't just refer to Langford's fondness for the verb "gaze"). Joseph Conrad could have written this in *Heart of Darkness*, but not Langford, who had the soul of a Kiwanian, not unless he was vouchsafed a moment of intense insight that few of those who have seen the falls since could ever recapture, not with cameras clicking and cell phones ringing on every inspiration point around.

Langford and the other early visitors saw the falls free of the ironic add-ons of the years; to them, "grandeur" and "sublimity" were not platitudes, but qualities they could grasp in their hands. That's what I found myself wanting to do—to see the park as clearly as those first visitors had, to get past the tourists, past the postcard familiarity, to take the grandeur and sublimity, even if they shook me, into my soul—and not apologize for using those words, either.

It's hard to see a celebrity place without the cliché haloes. When it came to Yellowstone's marvels, had I already reached the saturation point, one week in? Rudyard Kipling asked himself the same question on his visit to the park in 1889. "Miracles pall when they arrive at twenty a day," he wrote. "The power of the mind for wonder is limited."

This is exactly what I worried about at Inspiration Point, then again driving down through Hayden Valley toward the hotel. "Wonder"—theme for the day, theme for my trip, theme for the next stage of life. When I was young, I could stare at "wonders" for long minutes at a time, seeing them, focusing on them, realizing them, in a way I've seldom been able to do since. These weren't wonders in the world-class Yellowstone sense, but near-at-hand kinds of marvels. Views from the top of New England hills; the stars in a dark country sky; almost any trick of moving water; the leaves on maple trees in October, under which I would lie with my hands behind my head to stare my fill.

Somewhere along the way, somewhere in the course of daily living, the steady incrustation of responsibility, this ability to just sit and watch and wonder had become atrophied, even in me, a writer, someone who is paid to keep his eye fixed on marvels of every kind. Another visitor to the park, John Muir, took a bittersweet view of the problem. "As age comes on, one source of enjoyment after another is closed, but nature's sources never fail."

Okay, John Muir, I hear you on this—but the truth is that nature's sources *were* failing me, or beginning to. I could sense this happening; I told myself, well I can always go back to it, that kind of pure absorption in the moment. One day I'll retire to it the way other people retire to Florida. But here I was two weeks from turning fifty-five, and between this and that I hadn't gone back to it; my trips outside at night to stare up at the stars were becoming less frequent, the time I could happily sit staring into the middle distance was becoming shorter, even my love of music, my ability to concentrate on it, was much less acute than it had been when I was twenty, when you might think that the added years would result in just the opposite. Middle-aged people complain about "losing it," referring to strength, speed or stamina; this to me was minor when compared to letting the qualities and sights that make life more than endurable go flying on past without appreciating them.

Could it be pulled back again, a young person's sense of wonder, and, more to the point, could it be recaptured in a place that more than any other in the world justified its nickname—Wonderland? F. Scott Fitzgerald claimed that America was the last place on earth where humans came upon something commensurate with their capacity for wonder, and Yellowstone is one of the last refuges where you can test this capacity—and, for that matter, miserably fail.

A flagman stopped me along the Yellowstone, and I waited a half hour for construction trucks to pass. Beside me, the river looked cold and lonely, and I spent most the time in the fly-fisher's state of mild hallucination, seeing the rising rings of trout in what were probably only the surges and whirls tossed up by the current.

But then—eureka. Maybe it was the noise and ugliness of the trucks passing between me and the river—they were widening the road for the comfort of ever larger RVS—that crystallized my thinking. Between one moment and the next, brooding about these things, I realized I had stumbled upon one of the answers I had been on the lookout for, ever since entering the park. The primary reason I wanted to be alone in Yellowstone on my birthday was that I needed to be somewhere that would shake up my seeing, jolt me back to that sense of wonder I wanted very badly to recapture. I wanted to regain this *now*, so that I could enter the crucial years of late middle age armored with—and enhanced by—a talent that required neither money, nor equipment, nor elevated levels of fitness to achieve—the ability to focus on the grandeur and sublimity that comes . . . and this is the secret of youth that can be our secret, too . . . even in moments that are camouflaged and hidden by the weight of the commonplace. Been there, done that, seen those. Excuses for our jaded weariness, the three clauses that sink us. But maybe late middle age is the time to go back and see everything again, and really see this time, the Yellowstones and Yosemites of the near at hand.

Deep stuff—but that's why people go to Yellowstone in the first place, and who was I to break the tradition of two centuries? I was approaching the midpoint of my trip, and had done okay, caught some trout, caught some sublimity, and now here was a resolution worth all the time and trouble I had taken to find one. And I got to apply it that very night. The Lake area was quieter and more deserted than the other parts of the park; it had exactly the lonely, autumnal feel I had been looking for. The handsome Victorian hotel built on the lakefront wore its venerability well under the light clouds of evening, and there was my friend the lone buffalo, grazing under the pines by the fire escape, totally ignored.

As usual, I hardly bothered with dinner, just grabbed a sandwich and brought it out to a bench on the low cliff that fronts the lake. There can't be many moments during the season when you can have this view to yourself. Some trick of twilight made it seem that the sun was going down in the east over the Absarokas, and then I realized that what I was looking at was alpenglow, or something similar; it colored the ragged ridgelines into a soft gray-lemon color that, as the light faded, came down and touched the lake. Nothing stirred on the water, nothing beside the ripples and folds that moved slowly and stately across the surface, slanting ashore on the black gravel shingle below me with the softest, gentlest sound water is capable of making. Inside that softness was the secret of autumn . . . that's the effect it gave . . . and if I listened carefully that secret would be mine.

The silence, the light, the way those velvety folds seemed to flow from the mountains to take up residence in the lake. All these things, and then . . . the true surprise . . . my giving way to it, so for those few minutes I had what I had been looking for: forgetfulness, immersion, solace, oneness, not me looking down at the lake, but me and the lake together, unbothered, unvexed, unbewildered.

When I could no longer see the ripples, I went back to the hotel, shivering—and not just with cold. My room was the last on the endless corridor of the third floor, and it was apparent I was the only guest up there. I spent the night waiting for ghosts to appear, top-hatted gentlemen from the Golden Age of Yellowstone, or their bonneted ladies—not a bad feeling, sort of like waiting for the grizzlies, and it added a pleasant frisson that made me pull the blankets up higher around my chin. Near midnight I heard some bumps and knocks, got up to investigate—and yes, there he was, right below my room: the lone buffalo, red in the glow of the exit light, rubbing up against the siding for whatever companionship the old hotel could provide.

Two

MY PHONE CALLS HOME were always a little disappointing. I'd have so much to say, but with everyone so busy, off at school or soccer practice, I would end up saying it to the message machine, and my inability to talk with anyone (in the "real time" I still have a fuddy-duddyish affection for) started to get on my nerves. No more messages, I decided the next morning, but just before the beep went off, Matt picked up the phone. *Eureka!*

"What'd you say, Dad?"

"I said 'Eureka.' Now you say, 'Hi, Dad! Are you having a great time?'"

"Hi, Dad! Are you having a great time?"

"That's better. I am having a great time. Just a little while ago I was fishing this stream called Aster Creek, and three otters came swimming past, plunging up and down just like porpoises."

"Neat."

"Okay, your turn."

"We have a tournament this weekend, and we got stuck in the toughest division."

"Well, you're the hicks from the sticks. You can beat them in an upset; soccer can be a funny game that way."

"Here's Erin."

"Hi, Dad. What's that sound?"

"Elk. Here, listen. I'll stick the phone out the booth."

"Neat. Are you homesick yet?"

"It gets bad at dusk."

"Told you."

"How's school going? How's the college applying going?"

"Terrible."

"Why terrible?"

"I've got babysitting. Here's Mom."

Celeste came on—her bubbly spirits had no trouble jumping the 2,000 miles that separated us. She caught me up on the most important things . . . the kids were fine, the house was fine, there were no important messages . . . but just as I started to relax, she added one last thing.

"Your dad called. His anemia is worse, and now they're talking about giving him platelets."

"That doesn't sound good. Platelets?"

"It isn't, not for someone his age. He didn't want me to tell you."

"Has he settled into life at the retirement place yet?"

"He keeps saying it's for old people."

"Hear that elk?"

"Oh my gosh, it must be attracted to you."

"I'll call on my birthday, okay?"

"That's ten days yet. Call before. I'm driving Matt to soccer practice. Love you."

"I had a pretty special moment last night. I was—"

Click.

More than usually pensive, I drove south along Lewis Lake. I needed a trout, a big trout, to help focus my attention on the here and now. The outlet of the lake is said to harbor spawning browns in autumn, even some lake trout, and I decided, in the way fly-fishers do, that of course they would be waiting there, all excited, for me to come play.

I parked in the campground, high-stepped my way over and around a maze of blowdowns along an otherwise easy-enough trail. Lewis, big and windy, suffers in comparison to Lake Yellowstone, lying as it does at the bottom of a relatively flat basin. Its outlet, where the lake quickly narrows down to river size, is a lovely spot hardly anyone visits but fishers. As is the way in Yellowstone, an idyllic and gentle-looking meadow is given a weird twist via some random steam vents and patches of bubbling earth—they make the valley look like it's being slow-cooked in a crock—and, if the fish aren't in, it's still a perfect spot to sit and stare.

The fish weren't in—I knew that right away, even before stringing up my fly rod and trying a cast. It's a hard concept to get across to the non-fisher, but sometimes you can tell merely by the look of the water that fish aren't around; there's a green-gray color that makes the surface look impenetrable, unfathomable, and, in my experience, it's because the water, when it comes to fish, is totally empty. Still, I enjoyed the unhurried way the water flowed from the lake, then quickly gained momentum, as if sensing—and, wading, I sensed this myself—the dramatic, gloriously abrupt Lewis River Falls a short distance downstream.

I tried a few casts without expecting very much, stuck my hand down into the water and thought of warm soup. Brown trout deserve champagne, not minestrone. But so be it. I leaned my pack against one of the blowdowns, poured myself a cup of Earl

Gray from my thermos, stared out at the glorious scenery, and, in going down the list of all the subjects I needed to find some new perspective on while away from home, came to what was in many ways the most important.

There's a picture of Celeste taken when she was eleven or twelve. Smiling in the spontaneous way she's never lost, pigtailed, the parochial-school version of the All-American girl (she's wearing a white blouse, a green plaid jumper), totally unaware that she's pretty, totally at home in the moment, happy, confident, trusting, bursting with energy, to the point where you can all but feel her squirm as the photographer asks her, for the eleventh time, to sit *still*.

We have (and hide) a photo of me taken when I was a year or two older than that, on the uneasy edge of puberty. Huge head, horn-rimmed glasses, lips pressed thin in the way of people who are convinced they're homely—the only sign of hope or originality being that vivid red hair—the exact opposite, in every way that photographs are capable of measuring, from the bright, happy girl that was Celeste. If you hold both photos side by side, it's impossible to believe either child's future would permit even the remotest connection with the other.

These differences only widened as we grew our separate ways toward adulthood. While I've never figured out whether I became a writer because I was so solitary, or became solitary because I turned into a writer, the fact is that I spent my twenties as a full-fledged loner, with hardly any acquaintances, let alone friends. For a time, I was very much in danger of finding myself in the situation described by Edmund Wilson in his essay on Kafka. "He was too much at home in his isolation to be able to bring himself to the point of taking the risk of trying to get out."

Yes, I was too much at home there, the risk was very great—and then, by the very slimmest of margins, with just days to go before my sentence became permanent, I managed to escape through the bars—and only because by some miracle I found an accomplice, found this girl who had grown up in a totally conventional Massachusetts mill town, a cheerleader, Miss Congeniality, popular with the boys, a devout Catholic, someone who had never met anyone like me, but who, by some sudden, overwhelming intuition, decided that this reclusive, lonely man was the absolutely perfect one for her.

The power of love? For me, it's never been a cliché. To say that I owe Celeste my life is no exaggeration, but the most honest, sober, matter-of-fact statement I can make.

But gratitude, even eternal gratitude, doesn't carry you very far in marriage, not when financial pressures begin to squeeze, not when disagreements arise over the kids, or in those nasty moments of human irritability and pure cussedness when we argue over whose turn it is to wash the dishes. The dangers of living too closely with another human being, with knowing him or her too well, are very real. And yet the young person in me—which has lasted so long, has been so stubborn to quit, that I begin to suspect is the real me, the inner rock nothing is ever going to split—can never stop marveling at the trick of fate that went my way when I first met Celeste. The afterglow of that miracle, when I get to a certain threshold of restlessness and anger, always softens the way back to equanimity and acceptance. The princess kissed the frog—and the frog never forgets.

As for our differences, I think what they've done is given us jointly a wider base. Our wildly different backgrounds—a happy-go-lucky Catholic girl who was brought up not to ask any questions; a shy, earnest boy who, upon first hearing the phrase "non-conformist," knew that's exactly what he wanted to be—have allowed us to find an unexpected middle ground, where Celeste's genius for friendship and family and my modest abilities in the realm of ideas have made us, when it comes to facing the trials the world dishes out, a stronger, more formidable duo than either of us would be alone. Even our fights have largely been fights to understand each other; our victories are when, against all odds, we pull this off.

The same is true with the differences in our personalities. I'm sure the standard line about Celeste in town goes, "Oh, she's a sweetheart. A nurse, and so loving. Deeper and tougher than she looks, too. Walter? Well, he's, uh, *nice*, once you get to know him."

Differences, after time, can grate. Plenty of marriages have broken up because one spouse likes to talk over breakfast while the other demands silence. Our standard spat (and "spat" is the absolutely perfect word for these kinds of fights) involves Celeste's inability to say good-bye. Meeting a friend in the supermarket (hell—meeting a *stranger*), ushering a repairman toward the door, helping various nieces and nephews on with their coats as a long Thanksgiving comes to an end. She lingers over these moments for—minutes? hours? I can't say exactly because never once have I seen Celeste voluntarily relinquish someone by her own free will, even in what should be the most glancing of social encounters; it takes either the other person displaying enough closure skills to break free or, very often, me playing bad cop, stepping in to say, "Hey, it's late, we've got to go to get some shut-eye, thanks for coming, *hasta la vista*."

Celeste probably has a different interpretation of how this works.

And yet the truth is, I love this quality in her, even though it makes me irritable. ("Nice meeting you, good-bye," pretty much wraps up most conversations for me.) I married a woman with a generous, world-class heart. Who am I to complain when I see that heart in action?

Another big difference between us is our ages. Celeste is nine years younger than I am, which will make some readers snicker and nod, I suppose; how clever of Wetherell, to find a trophy wife the first time around. But just as our different backgrounds give us a wide base in human experience, our age difference gives us a pretty generous reach both ways into life's epochs, me being the pioneer out here advancing hesitatingly toward old age, Celeste with a foot, a spirit, planted back toward youth. I can warn her about what's ahead—and warn her frequently. She can remind me of what's behind—and reminds me often. Again, these differences seem to widen us, strengthen us, double us, not split us apart.

It says a lot about marriage in late middle age that sex doesn't seem quite the burning issue it would be at an earlier age. The "been there, done that, seen those" syndrome can rust a couple's sex life, just like it can tarnish everything else about the aging process. To an outsider, especially a young outsider, the most surprising thing is that for a couple our age sex can remain the strongest bond, even after all the repetitions. I remember reading articles when I was younger about how couples in their twenties made love an improbably high number of times a week, couples in their thirties significantly less, couples in their forties hardly ever. But that's another of those appalling statistics that don't really turn out to be so awful, not when you're in the middle of them, when being alone together once a week, rather than seeming like a cruel form of deprivation, actually becomes a tremendous joy.

You'd have to be pretty smug to brag about your sex life, but then, in this culture, you're apt to sound smug if you talk about your happy marriage at all. Humor may be the safest way. Freed of its procreative function, sex can get pretty funny pretty fast—as in the sexual mishaps and farces of early adulthood; but sex can also be funny as in the comfy old thing it can become in your fifties; and funny as in Viagra. But again, this is viewed from outside. As a participant, you learn that it's all very different—that after twenty years of making love with the same person, passion can still burn, desire can still make you weak-kneed, and intimacy still matters and counts for a lot.

Of course, if you sliced open a fifty-five-year-old man's sexual imagination, dissect it, and study it, you'd be in for a lot of laughs. It resembles nothing more than one of those condom machines found in truck stops or seedy diners, with slots marked "Sexy Novelties!" "Grab Bag!" and "Surprises!" For it *is* a grab bag, a wistful, funny, nostalgic collection that includes memories of past conquests that flit past your inner screen from out of nowhere, burn brightly for a second, then go out, often in the icy memories of major embarrassments you've been trying for thirty years to smother. There are the erotic stimulations that flash at you from almost everywhere in this culture—not arousing like they were when you were a boy, but semi-arousing, a kind of vague, ever-present sexual static too weak to actually make it to your groin. There are the burning embers that flare to life when someone pretty bothers flirting with you. A surprisingly long list of question marks, unsolved mysteries and exclamation points. A photo gallery of cheesecake nudes and Playboy bunnies shot through the scrim of time; a never-to-be-forgotten anthology of racy passages from *The Carpetbaggers* or *Peyton Place,* or those books you once found hidden in your parents' closet; half-formed fantasies that aren't richly detailed and novelistic like a young man's, but their abridged *Reader's Digest* version . . . harmless stuff for the most part, the random novelties and mementos sent to the brain by a sexual organ on its way from being a man's most restless, troublesome part, to becoming his wryest, most sentimental—or, let's face it, a character out of Doctor Seuss, one of those wizened, spindly old-sters remembering all the places it's been, the wonders it's seen.

There is one new and unexpected development. More and more our sex life has become a refuge from the outside world, not only one of our few entirely selfish moments during a busy week, but a preserve (a national park!) protecting us from the onslaughts of mass culture, the whiplashes of technology, the assaults of an intrusive government. Sex is becoming what it is in Orwell's *1984*: the only free act the proles are allowed, the one place they can forget Big Brother, the last corner of life where they can still be intensely human.

I've noticed—and you can add this to your endless list of human sexual peculiarities—that we tend to make love more often when the news of the world is really dreadful than we do when the news seems good. Do I mean to say that high unemployment numbers, government blunders, and natural disasters make us horny? No. But faced with the absurdities and horrors of the larger world, we cling to each other like drowning people clutching between them a precious life preserver, sex becoming—of all the things it might be at this age—the expression of the rebellious side of us, the dissident side, the defiant. The modern world, for its profit and power, tries to steal a lot from you as you age, but they can't have *this*—that's what loving couples can still find in each other's arms.

I'll say it as emphatically as I can. A happy, lasting marriage is as rebellious an act as a twenty-first century couple is capable of performing, with the tide of history dead set against it. Anarchists in the old days dismissed marriage as a hateful bourgeois convention, but if any anarchists are around who really want to throw a bombshell into society, my advice would be to construct a marriage that lasts. Divorce is the hateful bourgeois convention now—to resist it takes guts. Marriage is changing, and what it will become isn't clear; people are looking for ways to love each other in briefer, shorter spans. There will be lots of in-between states, continued turmoil, and a terrible rippling effect as fractures between couples widen into the community and cut away at foundations of every sort.

Am I ready to brag of mine as lasting marriage? I am going to defy superstition, risk smugness, irritate 50 percent of this book's readers, and answer *yes*, even though the future has all sorts of challenges waiting to trip us up. The kids leaving home, taking with them the focus of our joint collaboration; our parents passing on, the nakedness we'll feel when there is no older generation standing guard over us; retirement, being alone more with each other; financial challenges; health as an increasing concern. We're not so stupid as to think marriage will become any easier.

But I think a point in our marriage is already passed where all the things that might have split us apart now serve to unite us. The fissures become welds; the ice becomes glue; bonds are formed out of all the truces, reconciliations and apologies twenty years of living together necessarily entails. You can't survive the give and take of marriage without becoming oddly nostalgic toward the compromises that you fought your way toward and eventually found. That it is possible to occasionally hate someone you intensely love is the fundamental contradiction that you've either learned to accept by now or it's simply too late.

And the good times, they've been working on you all along, to the point where—married twenty years—you have a tremendous lot to look back on. A young couple brings to a marriage all sorts of dreams, and what's remarkable is that you wake up one morning to find to your complete and utter astonishment that the dreams are not out somewhere ahead of you anymore, radiant, alluring, and tormenting, but actually there in the fabric of your accomplished life, as real as bronze or silver or platinum, or whatever a twentieth anniversary is meant to represent.

Three weeks is a long time to spend in the park, compared to most people's twenty-four hours. But I was determined not to be rushed—to pick up one of the many glorious threads that compose the park and follow it all day, knowing I had plenty of time to follow another thread the next day.

I fished twenty rivers during my stay, plus two lakes, and I'm going to list their names here, for the sheer, evocative pleasure of saying them out loud. Yellowstone River. Gardner River. Lava Creek. Blacktail Deer Creek. The Lamar. The Firehole (Biscuit Basin and Muleshoe Bend). The Gibbon River. Hellroaring Creek. Soda Butte Creek. The Madison (Nine Mile Hole and the Barns pools). Cascade Creek. Aster Creek. Solfatara Creek. Ribbon Lake. Fan Creek (the lovely upper meadow). The Lewis River outlet. Straight Creek. Joffre Lake. Nez Perce Creek. Grayling Creek. Obsidian Creek. The Gallatin.

I worked out a good routine most days, up in the darkness to

make myself a cup of tea, off to the nearest lodge to grab breakfast and the makings of a lunch, a short drive to whichever river
I was concentrating on, carefully gearing up, the hike in to the
river, a hard morning's fishing, a long break for lunch, often in
the shade of the nearest aspen grove, then another river in the
afternoon, not fishing quite so hard now, more in the way of sitting and staring, quitting around six, then coming back to my
room to write in my journal.

The leisurely pace gave me a chance to do something that had
been on my wish list for a long time, which was to take a closer
look at Yellowstone's geysers. I'm probably the negative world-
record holder in this regard: this was my fifth trip to Yellowstone
and not once had I seen Old Faithful. I took a snobby, reverse
kind of pride in this. Old Faithful was the icon of the RV people's
Yellowstone, the tour bus Yellowstone, the prepackaged side of the
park I was determined to avoid. I was going to prove, by ignoring
its most iconic feature, that there was a hell of a lot more to the
park than just some tacky, over-praised bubbles.

This was foolish of me, short-sighted, but it set me up for the
best moments of the middle third of my trip. As well as splendidly
beautiful, Yellowstone is splendid in a loopy, weird, otherworldly
kind of way—a performance artist in the theater of nature's absurd.
Early visitors, almost without exception, looked at the hot springs,
geysers, mud volcanoes and paint pots, and thought automatically
of hell. (Cartographers in the 1890s had to go back and change
many of the park's original names, since too many contained
the word "Hell" or "Devil.") Modern visitors, conditioned in less
Calvinistic ways, tend to be immediately interested in the science behind these weirdly melodramatic effects, never mind the
portals-of-hell metaphors that scared our ancestors.

Old Faithful, I discovered, is great theater, just like they say. The enormous parking lot only had a few cars this late in autumn (things were so quiet that trotting along in the middle of the pavement, wearing a look of requited curiosity, was the only wolf I saw on my trip), and if not for three busloads of Idaho Falls school children, I would have had the geyser largely to myself. According to the clock in the visitor center it was thirty-one minutes before the next eruption. I stretched out in the shade of some lodgepole pines where not only did I have a good view of the geyser cone, I could watch the people waiting there on the horseshoe of benches waiting patiently to be amazed.

I counted ninety-one, mostly kids, but with a good sprinkling of seniors, many of whom, I noticed, held hands. About fifteen minutes before the eruption, dogs began getting restless—they looked up at their humans and made urgent little tugs on their leashes back toward the parking lot. At the same time, water began gurgling up from the bone-white cone, surges that slightly exceeded each other in what the rangers coyly call the "pre-play" period. The actual eruption, when it came, was both beautiful and anticlimactic; beautiful in that the strong northwest wind flattened the spray into rippling sheets of sideways-moving rainbows; disappointing since, because of the wind, the water didn't form that familiar, classic column seen in so many photographs on calendars and posters. And it seemed smaller than I had pictured it, smaller in the way Stonehenge seemed smaller when I first saw it, because I was looking at it through exaggerated layers of legend and hype.

I did better the next morning. Again, as with so many Yellowstone wonders, the trick is waking up early so that you can get them to yourself. I hadn't bothered looking at the visitor-center clock, so the eruption took me by surprise. I had crossed the little footbridge over the Firehole, climbed up along the boardwalk toward the Beehive and the other famous geysers, when I heard a whoosh and looked around—and there it was, Old Faithful blossoming into Old Faithful, high and fresh and sparkling, and no one there to see it but me.

I had big fishing plans for the day. I was going to concentrate on the Firehole, that strangest of all the world's trout streams, with active geysers on one side of you, boiling hot springs on the other—big plans, but I stayed around for three more eruptions, mesmerized, enthralled, converted. Why had I waited so long to become a geyser freak? All around me, as far as I could see, stretching across the valley toward the escarpment to the west with its fire-blackened trees, jets of steam shot skyward in the chill morning air. I wanted to laugh, to shout, to point—at no other time in my trip did I feel so strongly the need to have someone to share all this with. I realized, in that instant, how the most overwhelming imperative those first explorers had experienced must have been to immediately race back east to tell people about the wonders they had seen, even if they risked being called liars.

In the most inspired moment of place naming in U.S. history, General Henry Washburn and his exploring party of 1870 had named this great geyser not long after witnessing its repetitive trick. The words "old" and "faithful" had spontaneously come to their minds, when almost everything else they named in the park tended to be "Hell's" this or "Devil's" that. To these frontiersmen, it must have seemed the highest virtue—fidelity, steadfastness, dependability—and I thought how far we have gone in the opposite direction in the century and a half since, to the point where almost the only time you hear the word "faithful" now is in its sexual and entirely negative sense, "*un*faithful."

But maybe, I thought, as I watched each new eruption with its subtly different variation, it's time to restore "faithful" to its place on our short list of virtues, referring not just to faithfulness in marriage (though, quaint as it sounds, I see no harm in honoring it there), nor faithful in the religious sense, but meaning what I was watching here—referring to something that not only manages to be young and fresh and inspiring, but manages to be so right on cue. Stars are faithful in that sense, sunsets, even some heroic people who seem to draw upon a never-failing inspiration in the way that manages to be young and old at the same time. Fountain of youth, fountain of experience, drinking from both simultaneously? Yes, I was staring at the proof—young and old weren't necessarily opposites after all. It's an absurd thing for superheated water to suddenly pop its cork, but if it does this faithfully—every sixty-five minutes if its last eruption lasted less than two and a half minutes, every ninety-two minutes if its last eruption lasted longer than two and a half minutes—then you have something that serves, even in our sardonic age, as a tonic to our souls.

The next three days I was locked inside a smaller enchantment set within a larger one. The Upper Geyser Basin, Midway, the Lower Geyser Basin, the huge Excelsior Pool, the Grand Prismatic Spring. I shuttled between all of these, found it all but impossible to leave their radius. Even later, when I arrived home, that's what I ended up talking about the most. "Dad," Matthew said, with the expression that thirteen-year-olds get when they're leveling with you. "You've got geysers on the brain!" And he wasn't far wrong.

The visitor demographics changed during my time in the park. At first, it was the vacationing families, honeymooning couples and foreign tourists who flock to Yellowstone all summer, but each day further into October their ranks noticeably thinned. Fly-fishers, serious wildlife spotters, older couples (many attending courses offered by the Yellowstone Association or similar organizations)—they were the ones I saw in the hotel lobbies and cafeterias now, an unhurried bunch, breakfasting at nine or ten, letting the sun burn the mist from the landscape before venturing out to look for elk, trout or wolves.

I was surprised to find my mirror image among these—men my age traveling alone, bringing a book or map with them to breakfast, eating faster than they would have if they'd had a friend along, joking with the waiters and waitresses just for the sake of having someone to talk with after a little bit too much time alone. As far as I could determine, every single one of them was in the park to fly-fish. Good fishermen, better than me probably, and many had fished Yellowstone waters for years.

After a last sweep through the breakfast buffet, I sometimes overcame my shyness enough to walk over and join one of them for coffee. Rapport was instant—we shared information on which park rivers were fishing well and which ones weren't, then traded stories about rivers and streams all over the world. They are a well-traveled bunch, these autumnal fly-fishers. Still boyish, most of them, thanks to their fishing passion, but—and I don't think I imagined this—there was a partly wistful, partly bitter tone apparent in their voices when the subject strayed far from fishing. I put this down to the fact that most of them had retired from their careers too early, and not necessarily voluntarily.

The writer Jan Morris describes well what's at work here:

The specialist in retirement is a sorry thing. He potters around the house, he tinkers with this hobby or that. He reads a little, watches

*television for a half hour, does a bit of gardening, determines once more
that he really will read* War and Peace, *get to know Beethoven's last
sonatas or try a last time to get to grips with rock. But he knows that
the real energy of his life, the fascination of his calling that has driven
him with so much satisfaction for so many years, is never going to be
resumed. He no longer reads the technical journals, because they make
him feel outdated. He no longer goes to professional conventions. The
world forgetting, by the world forgot! What's it all been for, he wonders.
Sometimes he feels he is cracking up or fading out, and he avoids the
newspaper obituaries because . . .*

Talking with these fishermen, reading Morris, got me thinking
about another aspect of this strange landmark year. At fifty-five,
just when so many temptations begin seeming a degree or two less
tempting, there arises the most compelling temptation of all, for
someone who has worked hard and long at achieving something
difficult in life. At fifty-five, without blame, with dignity even, you
can give it all up.

At fifty-four, this seems all wrong. Someone who stops working
at that age has about them a tincture of defeat. Counseled out,
made redundant, outsourced, fired. This is what we assume has
happened to people in their early fifties who suddenly announce
their "retirement," and rather than congratulating them or asking
how they plan to spend their new leisure time, we're more likely
to ask how the job search is going. They're close to the finishing
line, sure, but their shoulders haven't quite broken the tape; they're
quitters, or at least it's tempting to think of them that way, men
and women who didn't quite have the stamina to complete the
grueling marathon that modern capitalism demands.

At fifty-five, thanks to the shelter of those two matching digits,

5-5, you can, without any such disapprobation, call it quits. Fifty-five has long been established as the legal and socially acceptable threshold for early retirement. Okay, it's a little early; sure, we sometimes wonder if the retirement was totally voluntary; yes, we expect the early retired to find another occupation to fill their lives, but that said, we're not surprised when someone packs it in at that age, we even envy them for doing so. "She's retired," a man might say, referring to a mutual friend who's just turned fifty-five. The word has a beautiful self-sufficiency about it; hardly any explanation is required.

Perhaps this explains the subtle sense of relief and safety I've long associated with the digits "55," even when I was younger. After all, what Sherwood Anderson wrote in 1924 still has relevance: "No American thinks of doing anything he enjoys until youth is gone; youth must be given over to money making and leisure is a sin."

Fifty-five is also the age, if you've been successful, when it's tempting just to coast. It's the age where you can become a professor emeritus, a senior consultant, an *éminence grise*, an old master—consolation titles that can often mask a brutal truth. While you may indeed retain the ability to do fine work, while you may still have the fortitude for the blood, sweat and tears, you now feel differently. Having fought so many battles through the years; having won some and lost many; having proved yourself so many times and found that you still had to go on proving yourself ad nauseam; having paid your dues to our Puritan work ethic; having completed, in a metaphorical way, your essential work in life, what you were put on earth to accomplish—having done all these things, you now find that between one birthday and the next you simply no longer have the desire anymore, hardly even the interest.

Worked there. Won this. Accomplished that. Again, the weary triad of the late-middle-aged. Whether or not to accept this and retire, counsel yourself out, or to persevere in the battle and keep working, is one of the toughest decisions a man or woman our age has to make.

But for every one who has the luxury of quitting, there must be nine or ten for whom early retirement remains only a dream. Fifty-five is not their threshold of freedom — it means at least ten more long years to work, maybe even more. (A new government report finds that personal bankruptcy filings are rising fastest for those sixty-five and over.) They're enslaved to credit cards, car payments are due, the mortgage has another fifteen years to run, college tuition has sapped their pension savings, one spouse has been laid off, alimony payments continue indefinitely, a divorced child needs help paying for day care, the price of gasoline goes nowhere but up. Retirement? Early retirement? Dream on.

Late middle age, for these poor souls, is mainly a matter of outlasting a truly stultifying boredom. They've performed the same task for over thirty years, perhaps, and while maybe they can make their hands do the chore one more time, or make their mouths repeat the same spiel, lecture or sales pitch, each repetition — is it up into the tens of thousands of times now? — chips away at something vital in their souls, so their jobs have long since become terms of indenture, jail sentences, hard time. These are the fifty five year olds who play the lottery, study the stock market, daydream about making a killing — not because they're greedy, but because they're desperately in need of escape. They fell into their jobs at twenty-one because they needed something, anything; performed it reasonably well through their thirties, though without much satisfaction; earned in their forties the perks and privileges you get by merely surviving, so it wouldn't be prudent to switch careers—and now, in their fifties, see it as something to tough out until the end. Boredom? The word is simply not intense enough to describe their punishment.

Boredom equals ennui in most people's usage, but in reality the two are very different. Boredom is the tired, listless feeling you get when you work at something you detest; ennui is the tired, listless feeling you get when you work at something you love for too long, or at something you used to love. It's not talked about much, but among creative people in their fifties some degree of it must be all but universal. Some suffer extreme cases intense enough to make them stop working; others find they must slow down or retool or go off in new directions, failing which, ennui—the creative laziness—gets the upper hand. Someone who's worked on an assembly line for thirty-five years and someone who's labored three decades with the power of their imagination, both cry the same tears over their beer.

To make a success of something creative—to invent, innovate, influence, inspire—requires so much in the way of endurance and sheer courage that it's not surprising that much of this can be used up by the time you reach fifty-five. Battle fatigue sets in; the shells and high-powered explosions you once charged through in splendid defiance now leave you cowering against the trench wall. You're not to blame for this—it's simply the way nerves work—but you blame yourself anyway. *Coward*, you say, though somewhat half-heartedly. In bad cases of ennui, you don't even have enough energy to loathe yourself like you used to.

Oh, you can still perform your work at a high level—there's a satisfying kind of nostalgia that comes with still being able to pull it off. The skill is there, the know-how, the smarts, but what is lacking is the desire, the willingness to take risks, fall on your kisser; what is lacking, most worrisome of all, is your wanting to do what it is you're good at doing. The fierce will to succeed is gone; people don't pat your success on the back anymore, but take it for granted; vanity has pretty much quit as a motivating factor; you've survived the bitterness that comes with your inevitable defeats (more visible to you, your toughest critic, than to an easily conned outside world), but you've found, post-bitterness, that the battle to surmount it has left scars of listless tissue; you're weary, to speak plainly now, of being brilliant, being creative, being smart.

Ennui on this scale is a luxury and an indulgence; many can't dip into it very far (surgeons, teachers, farmers) without doing real damage to how to our world spins. To fight it, you can play it safe, rest on your laurels, coast, though this only leads to more ennui and is hardly a solution. You can, if you're lucky, change directions within the same career, which might bring on that challenging newness that was one of the allures of your profession in the first place. You might switch careers entirely — an increasingly popular move, if you have the requisite flexibility and energy (and can transfer your benefits). Or you can retire early before the ennui festers, retire in dignity. It's the way many careers end now. Not with a bang, not even with a whimper, but a yawn.

Novelists, so the common thinking goes, never retire. Not for us the 401K plan; not for us a company-funded pension. We don't need it anyway, supposedly — we want to keep writing at a high level for as long as we can. The physical requirements aren't onerous; the mental skills, which are onerous, are said to be good in staving off Alzheimer's. "Retirement" is simply not a word a novelist would use, especially not with the adjective "early" placed in front.

But there is another kind of retirement, forced retirement, which is becoming more and more the inevitable terminus of many careers, including the novelist's. Yellowstone National Park, whatever else it is, is *not* the place to brood about the ups and downs of a writing life (though I did brood about this there), nor the current sorry state of serious literature. Suffice it to say that for writers interested in writing as an art form, for writers who feel the old way about literature, that it's the finest work in the world, part of an ongoing tradition and testimony that over the course of the last thousand years has brought humankind as much redemption as it's capable of grasping—people who feel that a story written by Anton Chekhov in Yalta in 1886 or a poem written by William Butler Yeats in Dublin in 1915 or an essay written by Albert Camus in Paris in 1948 has a direct, vital connection to our life and work—for people who feel this way, these are not propitious times.

Writers, like so many others now, can be forced to retire early from their vocation because their vocation simply ups and disappears. We're like typewriter sellers in this respect; one can be the best, most talented, hardest-working typewriter seller in the world, but what good is that when the world no longer buys typewriters?

The depression attendant upon this comes at a particularly vulnerable time. At fifty-five, anyone involved in a challenging career is having doubts about their abilities, worries about losing it, "it" being defined as the complex creative core that drives you on. Writers start fretting about losing it when they're in their twenties, so there's nothing new about this for me, except my worrying that, just as hypochondriacs can become ill, writers who worry about the loss of their creative juices can eventually lose their creative juices. Proust, who thought about this a lot, talks about the need to "restore some degree of movement to a spiritual machine which, after a certain age, tends to become paralyzed." Which is to ask, how long can you go on recharging a battery before that battery goes dead?

It turns out that this phenomenon has been documented and studied. Just before my trip, thinking about how listless I felt, wondering if this was my imagination's normal summer slump or something new and more worrisome, I came upon one of those newspaper articles that pop up exactly when you least need to read them.

Seems that scientists who specialize in "evolutionary psychology" have long wondered why it is that eminent male scientists—and male writers, male composers, and (especially) male criminals—all reach their peaks in their mid-thirties, then seem to experience an increasingly rapid decline in their abilities and output. "Dr. Satoshi Kanazawa, who has studied these patterns of male achievement, believe she has an explanation. Young men in any profession are driven to seek wealth and prestige because these attributes are attractive to women. Once men's urge to start a family has been satisfied, the wellsprings of productivity, whether in science, art or crime, run dry."

The article chews that over for a few paragraphs, then turns to a Dr. David M. Buss, who "agrees with the general idea that scientific productivity, writing and crime are all activities driven by men's pursuit of wealth and status." According to Dr. Buss, "Scientific and artistic endeavors are male attempts to compete for status and resources, though I don't think most men conceptualize it that way. Evolution has built in a drive for male competitiveness and status-seeking because it's attractive to women; there's no need for the drive to be conscious. The peacock tail is a flamboyant encumbrance of no help at all for physical survival, but of great value in seducing pea hens."

Opposing views are offered; one researcher points out, in apparent contradiction to this, that male income in the U.S. peaks at, yes, age fifty-five. Reading, I worried less about my writing urge being a subliminal kind of macho strut—anyone who writes serious literary fiction to impress the chicks is one messed-up evolutionary dude—than I did the chart showing male creativity declining after fifty-five. You immediately measure yourself against such graphs—a late bloomer, I would say that forty-six or forty-seven was closer to my peak—but that there has been a decline, not so much in my abilities as in my desire to exercise those abilities, seems incontrovertible. Changes in the outside world, the increasingly inhospitable cultural climate, account for some of this, maybe even most, but there's no getting away from the fact that some gradual slackening is beginning to undercut my imagination, my drive.

Any American brave or foolish enough to try to make a living off the arts probably deserves all the humiliation, neglect and punishment the culture dishes out. And yet there must be many people working in more conventional careers who feel exactly as I do—as if they've banged their heads against the same stubborn, unyielding wall for almost forty years now, their resilience is gone, and it's time to put an end to the heartbreak before it becomes permanent. People do not want to spend the last third of their lives shattered, embittered, aggrieved. If it comes to that—and this danger is very real—then perhaps it is time to retire, never mind that you're still working at the top of your form.

Declare your career a victory and quit. Declare it at least a tie.

For novelists, do a Melville or Salinger—retire from writing to please a public, and write to please yourself. If cultural changes are prematurely hastening our extinction, our extinction is still of a traditional pattern and falls within the harsh logic that has governed things for as long as humankind has engaged in mental toil—that eventually the world won't care for our work or need it any longer, and then it's time to make way for those who are young.

At sixty, I tell myself, I'll reappraise how things stand, though the truth is, in a writing life, the reappraisal, the constant redefining, starts the moment your career begins, and then it never stops. I am one of those lucky people who were born to do what they do; choice, though I kid myself about this, hardly entered into it. A calling *calls*. Stories form. Characters haunt me. My vocation, though I bitch and moan, is not quite done with me yet.

So now I will indulge myself with a very personal note, a pep talk to my soon-to-be-fifty-five-year-old self, one I will blame no one if they skip.

I remember, when discouragement strikes, the first time I ever read *Ethan Frome*, that much derided staple of high school English—of recognizing instinctively, though at fifteen I had no words for it, the artistic perfection of the tragic story, where not one sentence, not one image, is misplaced. Stoic Ethan Frome; his bitter wife Zeena; the girl he falls in love with, Mattie Silver. It brought tears to my eyes, not just because of the story's sadness, but the skill with which Wharton shows three people bound as tight as it's possible to be to their destinies, the perfect way she puts this down on the page. What could I do about the tragedy of their climactic sleigh ride once my crying was over? Some response was demanded of me, of that I was certain—and the only commensurate response was to conduct my life in such a manner that one day I could write such a tragedy myself.

How I longed for this! How I long for this still! There's the generalized longing to make sense of the world, or to frame its absurdity in such a way that at least the absurdity shines through. There's the longing for an idea (this nagging vagueness) to actually crystallize so work can begin. The longing to have the components of the idea fall into place, in meticulously crafted, tactically studied ways, on one hand, and genuinely spontaneous, unpremeditated flashes, on the other (and, for me, the more deliberate the craft, the more spontaneous the flashes). I long for the phrases to come, the sentences, the words, all of them in the right order, with the right cadence, the right evocations—evocations that are often doubled, a literal sense matching an allegorical sense. I long, writing a first draft, for the increased precision that comes with a second; writing a second draft, I long for the fussier precision that comes with writing a third—long to lie down on a couch with a pencil and, three drafts behind me, concentrate all my attention on each word. I long for the satisfaction and release of finishing. I long for the writing to last, to become something that can be read and reread in the future. I long, even as I finish, for the next idea to appear, the better idea, the one that will finally say, after thirty-five years of trying, what I was put on this planet to say—and so on and so on, morning after morning, year after year, century now after century.

From time to time one of the classier American magazines, rounding up some celebrity writers, will do an article on this theme: *If you could go back to any moment in American history as an eyewitness, what would that moment be?* I'm a sucker for these, read every word, since I enjoy playing that game myself. On restless, sleepless nights I have real debates with myself over when and where in this great five-hundred-year pageant of ours I would have a time machine plunk me down. Go for an obvious choice? Be standing lookout on *Pinta*'s tallest mast as America first looms into view? Stand by the little grove of trees in the Union center on the third day of Gettysburg? Or think locally? Choose one of the few times that world history ever visited our small corner of New England—the Battle of Valcour Island in October 1776, when Benedict Arnold, of all people, fought to a standstill a British fleet on Lake Champlain against a backdrop of brilliant autumn color?

These are the splashy, melodramatic choices, and perhaps it would be better to opt for something more subtle. Standing in the corner of his study when a weary but exultant Herman Melville writes the last words of *Moby Dick*? Watching in the wings during the first performance of *South Pacific* in 1949, listening to Ezio Pinza and Mary Martin breaking everyone's hearts? Or, on almost any occasion, watching Winslow Homer paint?

Editors, when they commission such articles, have learned that they have to rule out one bit of American history or else too many of their respondents will choose it: the Lewis and Clark expedition. And while I'd be tempted to sign on to the Corps of Discovery, their expedition lasted a bit too long, and to counterbalance all the drama of the voyage up the Missouri would be those winter months of boredom at Fort Clatsop.

A tough decision, this playing around with history, but I notice that I keep coming back to moments of discovery rather than moments of war. And within this wide heading, I would opt for a moment probably not too many even know about, let alone fantasize over—a moment that is so relatively recent and so relatively unheralded that it seems like I wouldn't be asking the time machine for a very big favor at all, to carry me back just that far.

If I could go back to one moment in American history—and this is not just because I was visiting the spot where it happened and so could save the time machine some gas—it would be to become a member of the 1870 Washburn Expedition to Yellowstone, the improvised, very amateur and yet tremendously important journey to the future park that was a unique combination of military campaign, Boy Scout outing, tourist excursion, and joint American epiphany.

I've mentioned the Washburn Expedition several times, but I should recap. After the Folsom party returned to Helena in 1869—the party which was reluctant to talk about what they had found in Yellowstone, not wanting to be branded as liars—enough of the story leaked out that a group of Montana Territory's most prominent citizens decided that now was the time to establish once and for all whether all the rumors were true. The prime mover seems to have been Nathaniel P. Langford (he who would wax so eloquently over the Lower Falls), an ambitious, well-connected man-on-the-make very typical of that time and place, though with some intellectual depth and more physical bravado than most men of his type. He had been in touch with robber baron Jay Cooke back in Philadelphia, who was trying to finance the Northern Pacific Railroad and was thus very interested in what promotable wonders lay along its projected route. It was a very American expedition in this sense—money was at the bottom of things—but in justice to the participants, plain old-fashioned curiosity trumped greed at every turn, and in the course of their journey they became conservationists almost despite themselves.

In the late summer of 1870 the nineteen-man expedition set out from Helena, led by Civil War veteran Gen. Henry D. Washburn; along with the enthusiastic amateurs came a cavalry escort commanded by ace Indian fighter Lieutenant Gustavus C. Doane. They remained in the future park until late September, exploring most of the marvels (they somehow missed the Mammoth Terraces), naming many features with names that have stuck to this day. On September 19, camped by what later became known as "National Park Mountain," they may or may not have jointly come up with the idea of establishing a national park to protect all the wonders before private entrepreneurs moved in and fenced things off. After returning to Helena, Langford went east to lecture about the wonders just as Jay Cooke had planned. It was these lectures, combined with newspaper articles written by other members of the expedition, that began the amazingly rapid drive toward the establishment of the park in 1872, with Nathaniel P. Langford as its first superintendent.

So. Hints about Yellowstone's marvels had by 1870 evolved from wild rumors into semi-confirmed reports. The Washburn Expedition was the first successful attempt to go into the future park and bring out the truth in a form (newspaper articles, lectures, primitive sketches) that could be transported to the settled part of the country and disseminated to a larger public who might soon be able to go there in turn. I can understand the motives of men like that, since, when you stop and think about it, they weren't that different from the motives that brought me to the park 130 years later. It's why I think I would fit right in with them, if I had the chance to go back in time. I would enjoy their curiosity; I would find the danger, modest as it was, stimulating; I would like their sense of responsibility and mission, leavened by their willingness to enjoy some fun. But most of all, I would value being among the very first to ever see the park's "unmanstifled" glories *as* glories. The parties that penetrated the Upper Yellowstone before this always seemed in a hurry, the wonders were mentioned almost in passing, and it's hard for a person today to have patience with this. "Move on!" one of the fur trappers or prospectors would always be shouting, maddened that I could linger so long staring into a canyon. With Washburn, the staring, the rapture, was exactly the point.

And what a cast of characters to camp out with! Reading about the early West is fascinating, largely because history's tide doesn't seem to have cast anyone up there who wasn't remarkably brave or remarkably prescient or remarkably weird. General Washburn, the leader, was only thirty-eight, but already dying of the consumption he had contracted in the war. As Aubrey Haines puts it, "His was a leadership which had no article of war for backing, but was, instead, based on reasonableness, genuine concern and a willingness to share every burden of march and camp." He was backed by the leader of the military escort, Lieutenant Doane, a larger-than-life figure who was a superb horseman and a crack shot—a man you can picture being played by Henry Fonda. Samuel Hauser was a businessman very much in the style of Montana businessmen of that period, someone who had a fierce ambition to wrestle his fortune from the potentialities of this newly won (or newly stolen) land; his motives, along with Langford's, were the most mercenary, and it's hard not to conclude that he saw in the expedition the chance to make a killing.

Truman Everts, at fifty-four the nearest to my own age, was a transplanted Vermonter who was very nearsighted—and whose myopia would win him a curious kind of immortality, when he became lost in the future park for a brutal thirty-seven days. Jacob

Ward Smith was a promoter, gambler, and lover of practical jokes, the one who saw the expedition as an extended party. His carefree attitude soon brought him into conflict with the sober Langford. In Haines's words, "Langford was dignified, scholarly, imaginative, introspective and very easily bruised, while Jake was boisterous, carefree, generous and an absolute realist."

It's fun to picture myself, not only dropped into the middle of Yellowstone's wonders at exactly the right moment in history to see them the clearest, but to imagine myself dealing with such extraordinary men. Several kept journals, and one more writer probably would have fit right in. This is what I played around with on my own little expedition through the terrain they loved. Eating alone in the cafeterias, waiting in my car for an afternoon hatch to get started on the trout streams, I would jot down journal entries on scrap paper as if I were a member of the expedition, a modern man plunked down in their midst, trying to understand the others and not make too great a fool of myself. I had fun with this, so eventually what began as a kind of imaginative doodling became something I did every day. Here then, in the spirit of Langford's classic account of the expedition, *The Discovery of Yellowstone Park*, is a sampling from the journal entries of that shyest, least-known member of the Washburn expedition, W. D. (for Dude) Wetherell.

Tuesday, August 23—Six days out and this is the first morning I've felt comfortable on my horse, the pain in my back and haunches having become so intense that it's burned the aches away—either that or I'm tougher than I thought. Amazing how horses—caring for them, feeding them, prodding them onward—is beyond all other concerns central to our day. Not just packers, but educated men like Langford and Hedges talk about nothing else; it's a bit like being plopped down among half-crazy NASCAR fans. Jake Smith had some fun with me this morning. He offered to switch horses for the day, loaning me his piebald which he claimed was "surpassingly gentle." Gentle, yes, but what Jake neglected to say was that his horse seems to suffer from an SAD-like depression, because every time a cloud crosses the sun and it darkens, he whinnies, kicks from side to side, bucks; my desperate attempts to stay mounted result in general hilarity among all. Lieutenant Doane, not surprisingly, given all the Westerns I grew up watching, is the one I admire most, though he's hardly deigned to notice me so far. He's not a military type at all, seems more sensitive and thoughtful than the others, though there's a presence about him, an obvious fortitude, that commands respect. We're camped tonight at the Boetler brothers' ranch, which is the only dwelling between Fort Ellis and our destination—a low brown cabin suggesting a pancake house or shoe outlet, every side covered with drying skins. Bear, elk, deer, antelope. What carnage!

Friday, August 26—Camped tonight on Antelope Creek, five miles from the Yellowstone River. Doane still scouting out to our east. None of the wonders we were led to expect are in evidence yet, but the country, to my eye, is beautiful everywhere. Not so the others. "Valley of Desolation" is what Everts wanted to call a pretty cottonwood-shaded canyon we rode through this morning, and I had to use all my eloquence to talk him out of it. A sibilant, rustling kind of noise at night drives the horses crazy—it's as if something were sucking in wet air and spitting it back out. Grizzlies? No one in the party seems to be particularly worried about them. Indians? Well, these they *do* worry about, and we take turns standing guard. Their prevailing attitude toward Indians seems to be contempt leavened with respect; take the fear away, and only contempt would be left. I draw the graveyard shift with Jake Smith who, to give him credit, can tell a good story. Most revolve around women. I'm no prude, but even so, it's pretty raw stuff. I listen, thinking, so *that's* what really went on in those bawdy houses and saloons. The airy whistling sound can be heard again off in the timber just before midnight. Hard to focus on, but with the fire whitening to ashes, it can't help making you think of ghosts.

Dawn now. While no one mentions the noises of last night, I notice Lieutenant Doane walking casually around our perimeter, as if merely stretching, yet making sure to check behind every tree for signs of—what? Nine days out and he's yet to address me a single syllable.

Saturday, August 27—What beauty! What extraordinary heart-stopping, overwhelmingly glorious beauty! Today, after a thick struggle with downed timber, we emerged into an open valley that extends for ten miles on all sides, leading up to an expansive, mirror-smooth plateau on the south and ringed on the east by the Absarokas. The Yellowstone is below us somewhere, though all we can see of it is the dark, puffy lip of its canyon. Swelling up from this is a plain of soft grass and sage just beginning to turn yellow and brown, lined with the most verdant green where the tributary streams plunge perpendicularly down toward the river, and tinsel-like threads of silver where the trees give way enough to reveal the water. The color shapes the sky, so, looking up (and finally I have a horse trustworthy enough to allow me to look up), I stare into an endlessly rolling plain of the deepest, richest blue imaginable. A forest fire to our west decorates all this with streamers of whitish gray, adds a cinnamon smell to the air that is not at all unpleasant. Elk graze completely oblivious to us; antelope stare coquettishly, then prance daintily off. What's odd, none of the others seem particularly enchanted with this, and they can't believe I'm lingering to stare when the wonders they've come for are still a half day's ride ahead. They came for nature's freak show, not this. *This* is the familiar landscape of their everyday lives, nothing out of the ordinary, and it's only my underfed, malnourished sensibility that finds extraordinary beauty here.

Made camp early near Tower Falls. The Yellowstone being low enough to ford, three of us waded to the east bank where we came upon the hot springs Doane had discovered earlier. *These* they got excited about, plus the furrowed cliffs just beyond. "Satan's Organ," Hauser wanted to call these, and I had to get up the nerve to tell him how truly awful a name this was. Smith ran over all excited, having witnessed the same cliffs from another angle and drawn his own inspiration. "Beelzebub's Parlor, we'll call it!" he shouts. Why are they all so eager to see this as hell and why does this only add to their enjoyment? It's too Puritan and deep for me.

Wednesday, August 31—After all the wild excitement, the waving of hats, the astonished pointing and gesticulating, the moment of stunned silence giving way to joyous shouts, all the wild talk about the Almighty and sublimity and the profound, those big words we threw toward Yellowstone's great canyon like pebbles tossed by little boys . . . after all the beauty that made us realize, if we didn't realize it before, that we do indeed have souls and that these souls can be overwhelmed with beauty and majesty and glory just as they can be overwhelmed by pain and suffering and despair . . . after all these emotions impossible to adequately write about . . . THIS. A sunset more majestic and stirring than any I've experienced before, as if nature were trying to show us that as beautiful a land as this is, it's nothing compared to what lies beyond, always beyond, tantalizing, tormenting, unreachable. A rainbow pattern, an arcing crescent, though the colors are not those you ever see in rainbows—amber, silver and rust, only softened by the haze of the forest fire so they seem more alluring than any purple, blue or pink. They undulate in waves as the sun sinks lower, but without ever losing their chevron pattern, amber nestled into silver nestled into rust. The top half of the sun seems to carry these waves on its back, and when it finally sinks below the horizon, with their support gone, the colors spread out and thin, so they extend as far as can be seen, north to south, a stain now, a magnificent chromatic wash.

Camped on the bank of Cascade Creek (cutthroat city, I'm happy to report) just before it drops into the canyon, and the homey sound of the rushing water drowns out the deeper roar of the Yellowstone Falls. Though it's nearly dark now, everyone in the party is still scampering around the rim of the canyon. When I left, they were trying by means of a rock and string to measure the height of the Upper Falls, all except Jake Smith; within fifteen minutes of our arrival at the Falls, he slapped his hands together, said, "Well boys, I've seen all there is, and I am ready to move on." The only one in camp besides me is our black cook who goes by the name Nute, and must be twenty-four or twenty-five. I've tried talking with him before, but he always seems shy of me—shy and gruff; he doesn't like anyone bothering him while he works, which I put down to his having a cook's fine instinct for self-preservation. Tonight I got him talking—with the canyon on one side, the sunset on the other, there were only the two of us to represent the human race, and so we *had* to talk.

An interesting thing. Except for General Washburn, no one in the party had much to do with the Civil War; most of them fled west to avoid it, and no one thinks the worse of them. Nute, on the other hand, was involved right from the start. A field hand in Mississippi, two plantations south of Jefferson Davis's, he fled north into Sherman's lines, made his way to Springfield, Illinois, enlisted in one of the first black regiments, saw fighting in half a dozen battles. Talks about this in the most offhand manner, as if it happened to someone else. "Oh yeah, Nute got a minié ball in his stir hand," he says, then, remembering it's *himself* he's talking about, glances down and seems surprised that the scar is still there, like a wrinkled doughnut hole covered with a flap of dough. I ask him what he thought about the Lower Falls. "A powerful mess of water, yes sir," he opines, but he's playing a role for me now, one he doesn't enjoy, because that's the last thing he says—he's back over his cooking fire now, getting grub ready for the boys when they come back.

One of Doane's troopers, Private Moore (an accomplished sketcher, the only one in our group) comes back and tells me a story that tops all the others. He had climbed a short way down the canyon's rim, trying to find an even better vantage point from which to see the falls, when he heard a huffing sound directly above him. Jake Smith having some fun with me, he decided, but when he spun around he saw it was a young grizzly snuffing its way along the rim looking for pinecones. Before Moore could shout, the grizzly saw him and jumped sideways, startled—jumped sideways, lost its balance, skidded on the rocks, and went sailing head over heels into the canyon. Moore, who hadn't time to be afraid, felt an immediate surge of pity, as if it were a man falling. The bear grew small and smaller, and was out of sight entirely before—far, far below in the gray-green torrent—there was the briefest of vertical interruptions, then the river roared on.

Sunday, September 4 — Camped on a grassy shelf overlooking Yellowstone Lake. Camped with nineteen stark-raving-mad gun nuts, to be precise — they're all out there right now, even Nute, taking turns shooting at empty cans of peaches which they toss out into the lake. They can talk for hours about horses, but that's nothing to how they can talk about guns. Poster boys for the NRA.

Elk for dinner tonight, compliments of Lieutenant Doane who felled a buck at an improbable distance and was immediately mobbed by the others like he had just won the World Series with a walk-off home run. In front of our camp is a wide beach like you would see on Cape Cod, and it extends for miles in either direction right around the lake. Not sand, not exactly, but something darker and grittier, and yet it yields pleasantly under your boots. This beach, which must run for 150 miles around the lake's circumference, fascinates me more than the mud volcanoes the others raved over this morning or the odd sandstone formations that litter the sand with all kinds of weird and suggestive shapes, from small clay pots to perfectly formed barrels. I think that here I appreciate the vastness of this land, its physical immensity, whereas elsewhere, along the canyon, say, I think more about the immensity of time. But whatever force made these beaches did so with joyous, slapdash extravagance.

(Later.) The others went to bed early, but I stayed up late talking with Everts about places we both know in Vermont, and after he went back to his tent it was my turn to stand guard. Again, and more vividly than ever, I felt a lurking presence just beyond the reach of the campfire's light, something that is too shy to draw closer, but too curious to disappear. I'm still tempted to call it a ghost, but it's even more incorporeal than any ghost would be, even more nebulous. And it's not necessarily hostile to us either;

whatever it is, it's staying neutral, and seems to be content now merely to keep us company, a silent, unseen member of our expedition. For lack of a better word, I'm referring to it (only to myself of course) as an *idea*, or the ghost of an idea. I would put it down to my overactive imagination, but I'm positive that Doane senses it, too. He strode over to the fire at midnight, and this time I was sure he was going to break his reserve and actually talk to me, but no. He walked through the light and disappeared, though I could hear quite distinctly his footsteps as he circled our perimeter, trying to grasp—in his stolid, no-nonsense way—what, though with great difficulty, I'm sure now *is* graspable.

Monday, September 5—I lost it this morning, big time. The others enjoy teasing me about fishing, claim it's the only subject I ever think about, treat me as half-demented, which I either have to go along with or suffer their worst condemnation, being labeled "stuck-up." And so Jake Smith came up to me this morning while I was splashing lake water in my face; he stuck a willow branch in my hand, ordered me to catch some trout for breakfast. "Sure, no problem," I said, swishing the branch back and forth like it was a fine Winston fly rod. "Only I need your advice first, Jake. These cutthroat aren't as dumb as you might think, it's going to take matching the hatch to bring one in. You think I should begin with a Baetis, say possibly a crippled Baetis with a parachute wing tied on a size 22 hook? Or maybe go deep instead, try a black-sparkle Wooly Bugger or a hare's-ear tungsten Bead Head Nymph? I could go caddis instead, but I think they're on midges, so maybe a size 24 Griffith's CDC gnat fished on a 7X tippet so I don't spook 'em?" Smith stared at me as if I was raving in tongues. My anger cooled then. I shrugged, pointed back toward the campsite. "Get me a good hunk of bacon, Jake, and I'll catch you a mess of trout."

Saturday, September 11—The decision was made to follow the lake's eastern shore so we can intersect the Yellowstone at its unknown source. While no one regrets our boldness, we're paying for it now. This is the most difficult terrain I've ever experienced, thanks to the thousands of blowdowns, fallen trees, many half-burned, which our horses have to climb over or around to make even the slightest, most grudging progress. It's as if the land, so generous before with its wonders, is now teaching us how utterly hostile it can be—a lesson drummed in this morning when we awoke to find bedrolls, saddles and grub boxes covered in eight inches of fresh snow.

Climbed a low mountain with Langford this afternoon during one of our stops; where the trees gave way we saw the lake spread out in all its vastness, and mountains to the south that Nute tells me are called the Tetons. In a muddy spot by the lakeshore we came upon the trampled imprints of unshod horses. Doane attributes this to a party of Blackfeet, and guard has been doubled tonight.

Named my first feature today! We crossed a particularly pretty little brook that bounced down into the lake. Hedges and the others, at the breaking point from all the blowdowns, wanted to call it "Devil's Washboard," which was the worst name they've come up with yet. I suggested "Chipmunk Creek" for the little critters that hopped over our legs during lunch, and this time I won.

Monday, September 12   During our journey almost everyone has been lost for an hour or two, some for as long as half a day, and this morning it was my turn. I stopped to fish a little tributary, and when I tried to catch up with the others I couldn't find their tracks. A moment of panic—this was not very pleasant—but then, remembering my old Boy Scout training, forcing myself to remain calm, I came upon horse poop, warm and fragrant and reassuring. From Blackfeet horses? An interesting question, but almost immediately I came upon Nute and the slowest of the pack train.

Five o'clock now. Everts has not come in. We compare notes, but none of us remember having seen him since morning. It's decided to send a party out to find him, but it's too late for that now, and though we fire shots to let him know where we are, yell at the top of our lungs, he will have to get through the night on his own.

Monday, September 19—The guilt over leaving poor Everts behind has cast a pall of gloom over the entire expedition. We left food for him at a prominent spot, marked a trail showing which way we've gone, but it's hard to imagine he's still alive after the bitter cold of the last five nights. We think to ourselves, well, he's either lost his glasses and can't see, stumbled into a hot spring and been scalded, or been scalped by a raiding party of Blackfeet, while we *tell* each other, well, he's probably managed to follow the Snake River down toward the settled areas and is now eating better than we are, laughing at his misadventures. But with food low, the weather turning, we can't linger here any longer. On top of that, everyone was feeling weary and homesick—until this afternoon. We were convinced we had pretty much seen all the wonders this Yellowstone land is capable of exhibiting, and then, in one remarkable instant, realized that all the wonders were only just beginning. I happened to be at the head of the column riding beside General Washburn, listening to his strictly confidential opinions of U. S. Grant. We had been following what we assumed was the Firehole River for the last hour, but it was a rocky, shallow stream, nowhere near as remarkable as we'd been led to believe. All the greater then was our astonishment when, coming out through the edge of the heavy timber, we entered a huge lava-white basin, and just at that moment, with timing so melodramatically perfect I hesitate to write it down, a huge column of silver-white water burst skyward a hundred feet right before us, forming a high airy column that blossomed at the top like a watery tulip. A geyser! And not just one geyser, but, as we leaped from our saddles and began running, a hundred more of them jetting skyward on every side. Ten minutes later, ten minutes of rapturous staring and excited shouts, and we had all agreed that these formed the greatest wonders of our trip.

Wednesday, September 21—This will be our last full day in Yellowstone country. Several hours of fast traveling will bring us to the valley of the lower Madison and twenty-five miles further the mining settlement of Virginia City. But it's of last night's events that I must write. After a day spent exploring the geysers and hot springs, naming the most prominent, we camped in a beautiful meadow near the base of a rampart-like mountain where the Firehole enters the Madison. No one stood guard. It was impossible to believe, amid all these wonders, that anything could possibly harm us, and so for the first time we all sat around the campfire together, even the packers, even Nute. And what a fine, towering fire we made—a geyser of flames. In its light, all the stubbled, emaciated faces looked feverish and red, though all the more vivid and earnest for that reason. It made me think of a council of Viking elders, or Ulysses and his men, something epic, a scene that stood outside time.

Someone, I think Hauser, suggested that we utilize our explorations to obtain quarter sections of land at each of the prominent features—that we divvy everything up and thereby make our fortunes. Thousands would come from all over the world and be willing to pay to see such miracles, of this there could be no doubt. Someone seconded his idea, suggested that we put our names in a hat and that lots be drawn to see who would get the canyon, who would get the Lower Falls, who would get Yellowstone Lake and so on. There was some hesitation—a few were sensitive enough to see this was a bit hasty—but in general everyone went along, and Hauser (all but salivating now) had started to write names down on paper when I got up the courage to have my say.

"Or we could do something else," I said, pitching my voice to go under the fire's crackle. "We could do something very different."

With what can only be described as a look of joint, collaborative astonishment, all eighteen of them turned and stared at me. What was this dude, this tenderfoot, this easterner going to say? For that matter, how dare he say anything?

I only had a few seconds to grab them. I knew I had to keep it simple and yet make it breathtaking. I needed to get their attention and hold it with something so grand it would blast away their cupidity and selfishness, and expose the bedrock of their better nature. A sound byte was needed—twenty-first-century technology the pithy power of which, in their wordy, grandiloquent world, they had never been subjected to before.

"We could insure this whole region is protected forever for the pleasure and edification of the country at large. We could create a gigantic park here, or commons, so these wonders are never despoiled or exploited for one man's profit. We could fight so hard to create such a park that posterity would remember and bless us forever."

They leaned toward the fire, as if they meant to pick up brands and hurl them at my forehead—what I saw on their faces I misread as outrage or fury. I thought of the old movie *Twelve Angry Men*, where Henry Fonda is the lone holdout on the jury and must convince the others one at a time. Who, if anyone, could I convince first?

Cornelius Hedges, as it turned out. After what seemed a very long time, he finally nodded, nodded gravely and judiciously, as if he had been giving just this subject a great deal of thought.

"I agree. It's only natural that men in our professions think of profit first. But this is one land where profit should have no place."

Langford came around next, perhaps remembering Jay Cooke's railroad and his part in promoting it.

"This should be a resort for *all* Americans."

Then, very quickly now, the others (except for a red-faced Hauser, who looked like he would explode) all chimed in. A wonderful idea! One that would not only do a great deal of public good but would make the territory of Montana a Mecca for visitors from all over the globe! We could write articles around the idea, lobby congress, start the ball rolling. I got so caught up in their enthusiasm that I even rashly promised to write a book.

Thursday, September 22—Deepest autumn now. The elk bugling, the aspen leaves gold, the frost in the morning enough to make us reluctant to leave the warmth of our sleeping robes. The last morning of our adventure. Today, by separate paths, we return to the settled territories. Had a surprise at breakfast. Langford, who has mostly ignored me, came up and asked if I would be interested in reading his diary entry from last night.

"Nothing would please me more," I said. Here, sitting on the stump of a lodge pole pine, is what I read.

The proposition was made by some member that we utilize the results
of our exploration by taking up quarter sections of land at the most
prominent points of interest, and a general discussion followed. Mr.
Wetherell said he did not approve of any of those plans—that there
ought to be no private ownership of any portion of the region, but that
the whole of it should be set apart as a great national park, and that
each one of us ought to make an effort to have this accomplished. His
suggestion met with an instantaneous and favorable response from
all—except one—of the members of our party, and ever since the
matter was first broached, our enthusiasm has increased. I lay awake
half the night thinking about it; and if my wakefulness deprived my
bed-fellow, Mr. Wetherell, of any sleep, he has only himself and his
disturbing national park proposition to answer for it. Our purpose to
create a park can only be accomplished by untiring work and concerted
action in a warfare against the in-credulity and unbelief of our national
legislators. Nevertheless, I believe we can win the battle.

(Later). Sad to think that this miraculous moment of time travel
will soon be over. The others complain about the distance left to
return to their homes, but it's nothing compared to the journey
back that I face. We were resting near the Madison, skimming
rocks across the rocky shallows, and I walked off by myself to try
to come to terms with what I've seen and experienced. And what
was odd is that this was the first time on the journey that I didn't
sense that lurking something following us, watching us, apprais-
ing us from the near distance. A ghost or an idea or whatever I
tried unsuccessfully to label it. And I realized only now that it was
gone, that this *had* been an idea, all right, a good idea, a wonderful one, and it was only last night as we grasped it around our
campfire that it was content, its mission accomplished, to leave
off its haunting.

I wasn't the only one to understand this. As I turned to go back to the horses, whom did I see, walking further out in the woods as always, but Lt. Gustavus C. Doane. He seemed to be listening for something inaudible off in the distance, then, stopping, he nodded vigorously to himself up and down. It was gone for him, too, the haunting. We had exorcised it by making it real.

He saw me. He walked over, and for the first time on the expedition extended his hand. But still, he didn't say anything to me, not directly. Instead, he turned and rose up on tiptoe, and squinted as if to see as far into the future as he could.

"The beauty," he said, his strong voice quivering. "The beauty!"

Three

IF THERE WAS ONE disappointment during the first two weeks of my stay, it was Yellowstone's weather. Not that it was bad—it was far too good. Each morning when I went out to my car, the frost would already be slurring down the windshield, and by ten the sun burned strong enough in a cloudless sky that I was splashing sunscreen all over my face, stuffing my fishing vest with water bottles to keep myself hydrated, eyeing the river for shady spots where I could rest. On one day, the temperature hit 93, a park record. I'd seen some warm weather on earlier visits during the summer, but then the inevitable afternoon thunderstorm cooled things off. Now, in October, there were no thunderstorms; the sun was so brilliant, so annoying in its brilliance, that I began thinking of the adjectives "pitiless" and "harsh."

The hot weather bred wariness in the park's creatures. The bear and (except at Mammoth) the elk stayed high in the alpine meadows where they weren't easily spotted; the bison, asleep in the high sage, stayed three-quarters out of sight; the trout were nervous and flighty, and a fly line landing on the water would send them fleeing in panic. This last bothered me most, since I had come out there hoping for great autumn fishing. Cold, cloudy weather would send spawning browns migrating into the park from Hebgen Lake, but this balmy sunshine kept them prudently at home. Cloudy weather would also help the mayfly hatches; mayflies, the small Baetis, rise from the gravel of the stream bottom to the surface, dry their wings before taking flight, and on sunny, warm days their wings dry so quickly they're hardly on the water long enough for the trout (and the fly-fisher) to find them.

Wary, everything in the park was wary, including me. This is not an era where we look at delightful weather with unadulterated delight. Somewhere in my restless reading of every pamphlet, brochure and book I could find dealing in any way with Yellowstone's future, was a printout from the Natural Resources Defense Council spelling out how exactly these record temperatures might affect the park. More pest infestations (the whitebark pine, whose nuts are Twinkies for grizzlies, might soon disappear), diminished snowfalls, more intense wildfires, a 5.4-degree increase in summer temperatures that would pretty well finish off the trout. It wasn't pretty reading. Yellowstone's creatures would have to find a way to migrate north from their isolated island to a colder climate, the article said—which left me with a ludicrous image of grizzlies, elk and bison standing by Highway 287 with their overstuffed valises, paws and hooves extended, hoping to hitch a ride with the trucks.

Climate change spells bad news for Yellowstone, and bad news for us all. The article ended with a somber nugget, a scientist's prediction: "The earth is going to become an ecological disaster, and somebody will visit in a few hundred million years and find there were some intelligent beings who lived here for a while, but they just couldn't handle the transition from being hunter-gatherers to high technology."

So it was the end of civilization that was written in that remorselessly sunny script, not just a bad case of sunburn or confusion to the trout. For me, a comparative stranger to this climate, change was harder to measure than it was at home in New England, where there was abundant evidence that things were cooking at a much faster rate than even the most pessimistic experts predicted. Our first frost came in mid-October now, not the first week of September as it always used to. Farmers could sometimes still hay in early December. Our maple sap started running in early February, not March. January days, more than a few of them, were so warm that our teenagers wore shorts. Smallmouth bass spawned two weeks earlier in the spring. Anyone with even the most cursory involvement with nature could see that New England, with character that had always came from its climate, was softening up.

Here in Yellowstone, perhaps because I was on vacation, I was curious more than alarmed. This was not the autumn weather I expected, and this disappointed me, but didn't scare me out of my wits. Then, too, the sun was making its own more immediate point—the clothes I had packed were too heavy for the weather. After yet another day wearing the sole summer ensemble I had brought (thin nylon hiking pants, thin cotton fishing shirt), I decided to drive to West Yellowstone the next morning and make a raid on a T-shirt factory. That night, restless and not sure why, I heard thunder in the distance, and then rain pelting down on the cabin roof, heavy rain, serious rain, and I knew that real autumn had come to Yellowstone at last.

It was still drizzling in the morning. The geysers around Old Faithful seemed involved in heavy lifting, to make an impression on the clouds that pressed down. The ceiling was low; only quarter slices of the surrounding ridges were visible. Humidity is a quality

you simply don't associate with Yellowstone, but it was so humid
that, for the first time on the trip, a short hike to the river left me
sweating. This was the Lamar, over in the northeast corner—my
favorite wedge of the park, and one I was curious to see in the rain.
What struck me hardest was how maritime everything seemed
there—I could have been fishing in Newfoundland or Labrador.
The landscape wore that intimate, drizzly kind of self-containment
you see in the high latitudes near ocean, the swollen perspective
of things near at hand, so a small rock off in the distance looked
like a buffalo, and a small hillock was inflated into a mountain.
Yellowstone is usually about grandeur, and small details can get
lost in that, but not in this weather. Secrecy, intimacy, particulariza-
tion—these were the words I jotted down in my notebook, trying
to capture a quality that was brand-new to me here and difficult
to pin down. The clouds formed a plateau above Yellowstone's
own plateau, and between them every feature seemed awash in
significance, so the park's wonders were tripled.

The wetness had a soothing influence on the park's wildlife.
Until now, they had stayed shyly out of sight, but on the drive over
to the Lamar I had my best hour and a half of animal spotting
on the entire trip. In the wide Gibbon Meadows, three bull elk
had drawn a roadside crowd. One, the largest, claimed a penin-
sula of marsh grass on one side of the river, and the other two,
younger males, stood on the other bank respectfully out of his
way. There was no sign of any harem—clearly, the big bull had
some evolutionary weakness that the females, showing natural
selection, were savvy enough to stay away from. He was a lonely
figure. That wide rack of antlers: what use were they? Meanwhile,
on the swampy side of the river, the two young bucks suddenly
remembered what their own antlers were for; they lowered their

heads, took a few tactical steps backward, then ran toward each other and exuberantly butted, giving off a clattery, metallic sound that suggested dueling broadswords. Over and over they did this, throwing up bright skirts of spray that left we spectators oohing and aahing.

That was for starters. Near Mount Washburn, I came upon a roadside grouping of one of the park's shyest animals: bighorn sheep. No nervy tightrope walking along cliffs for this bunch—they seemed happy to be on level ground, and nibbled placidly on the putting-green-smooth grass that grew along the road's margin. I spent twenty minutes with them before they moved off (twenty minutes that allowed my brakes, overheating, to completely cool)—a highlight for the day, certainly, but nothing compared to what happened next. I was halfway around Mount Washburn, coming out on a drop-dead spectacular view just north of it, where the valley suddenly unfolds and then folds again, becomes rimmed with rank after rank of ridges and mountains, when I noticed the passenger in the van ahead of me turn and excitedly point. They were going too fast to stop, but, warned by her signal, I pulled over, looked the way she pointed, and immediately saw my first Yellowstone grizzly, fifty or sixty yards up an open slope to my right.

This was the briefest of encounters—the grizz was moving along with definite purpose, perhaps heading toward a cache of those whitebark pinecones that biologists worry may soon disappear. Its coat was the same tawny color as the meadow grass, and its hip muscles rippled the way the grass would have if there had been any wind. I had seen grizzly bears before—there was a close encounter once in Glacier when on a family hike—but this was my first Yellowstone one, and it stirred me deeply. Watching him, I had the same kind of reaction I get when I come upon a celebrity on a city street—my god, they really exist after all!—and my first instinct was to call my wife and tell her all about it. But no movie star, no sports celebrity, no anchorman ever walked with the confident self-possession this grizzly displayed. *My home, not yours!* his carriage suggested. *My home!* I watched him for perhaps fifteen seconds, and something in the dignity and ease of his presence got that message across quickly.

The rainy, colder weather had a stimulating effect on the trout. Over the next few days the fishing improved dramatically, as spawning browns began moving into the park from Hebgen Lake just beyond West Yellowstone. This operates much like a spawning run of salmon; the brown trout, born in the Madison or its tributaries, the Gibbon and the Firehole, run down to Hebgen as juveniles, grow to maturity there, then come back to spawn in the same stretch of river where they were born. They're often accompanied by big rainbows, who won't be spawning until the following spring; they like brown trout eggs, and some of them, the evolutionary hard chargers, probably feel the need to get established before the less adventurous fish join them in the spring. These rainbows and browns are often *big* fish; at home in a good trout season I might catch one fish over twenty inches, but now, with the return of the spawners, I had a crack at four or five fish that size every day. Even if I didn't manage to land them all, it was still tremendously exhilarating, like suddenly graduating from neighborhood Wiffle ball games to Yankee Stadium.

Exhilarating, for that matter, just to be in their presence. So much is migrating *out* from the park in the fall—the buffalo think about roaming dangerously northward; the elk wander out into the path of hunters; the tourists begin to depart; the geese head south—that it's nice to be around a sizeable chunk of nature that wants *in*, and wants in very badly. Smart fish, to understand, at some level, that they're swimming toward the safety of America's oldest national park. Being attached to one, or just seeing a huge fish resting in the shallows, awakens that atavistic satisfaction that is half the delight of fishing. Big fish always get our prehistoric juices flowing, but what gets the adrenaline pumping fastest is to be around run-up fish, seasonal migrants, who, once upon a Paleolithic time, appearing out of nowhere, supplied our ancestors with as much in the way of riches as they surely ever knew.

No sign announced the browns' arrival in the park, no gong went off, but there was an unmistakable signal I had no trouble deciphering. Until now there had been hardly anyone fly-fishing the thirteen-mile stretch of the Madison in the park, but now I saw a half-dozen on the upper meadow alone, and not just any fly-fishers either, but the serious ones, driving battered trucks with Montana plates, apt to be smoking stogies as they splashed by me in the shallows, intent and motionless when they eventually got to where they were fishing, as proud and immobile, from that distance, as Easter Island statues, with the same kind of intent, forward-leaning slant.

A migration of its own, if you stopped and thought about it (and for many fly-fishers, the signal to move into the park must have come digitally, via the Internet). Like spawners, we paced ourselves to a diurnal rhythm—apt to be active in the morning and again late in the afternoon, but resting in some comfy sheltered spot during midday—and like spawners we were wary of the competition. If there was another fly-fisher approaching our favorite hole as we approached it ourselves, we exchanged baleful stares, made little bluff charges at each other (or at least wanted to), and then the weaker or nicer one would shrug and move off to fish somewhere else.

But there are currents in fishers just as there are currents in rivers, and if you wait your chance, unexpected openings occur and you can fish where you want. I went into the Gibbon just above Madison junction, kicked through the ankle-deep water over to the choppier Firehole, walked its bank toward the canyon where the gradient steepens, and started fishing. My careful probing of the pockets and pools resulting in nada, I tied on a big Wooly Bugger and played the chuck- and-duck game instead, tossing my fly out as far as I could across the heaviest current and letting it swing downstream. I had a hit immediately, felt the depth of a very good fish, then, before I could stop and do anything about it, felt the line go slack.

Interesting. I walked back upstream and started over. This time I was ready, and the next trout, when I landed it, turned out to be a gorgeous, butter-colored brown, just shy of twenty inches. It's always that first fish you value most. One of the reasons I migrated to the park in autumn was to be connected to *this* autumnal migrant that, for the brief second it took to unhook it, lay cradled in my hands just beneath the water's surface. *Connection*—that favorite buzz word of our times, and here was connection as literal as you could make it, and if it had come via something with the absurd name "Wooly Bugger," well, that only added to the magic. I released the fish—but the connection held.

Later in the morning, driving downstream, I stopped at Nine Mile Hole, which forty years ago was probably the most renowned stretch of the Madison in the park, a half mile of river made famous by legendary fishing writers of the past. The currents governing who fished where again flowed in my favor; for an hour I had the boulders, the log jams, and the weed-covered lava shelves all to myself. This paid off very quickly. I was throwing my Wooly Bugger downstream toward where a raft of flotsam and jetsam thickened an already huge boulder, and when the fly arced through the sweetest of sweet spots just upstream and to the left of the logjam, a very good fish took hold. I hooked it—surviving those first terrifying moments when the fish shook its mighty head—and then we proceeded to dance a frantic little dance, the trout trying to get under the logs, me doing everything I could to persuade it to swim toward the bank.

There can be some brutality involved in landing a big fish. At times during our struggle, with the road so close, I felt like a molester trying to bundle an innocent victim into my car. But then the little-kid fun kicked in, and I was laughing out loud (or at least audibly chuckling) by the time I wedged the trout between the grassy bank and my waders, twisted the fly out, and let it swim free. It was twenty-two inches long, and with probably five pounds of fat and muscle—a female this time, swollen with eggs. I wasn't chuckling from insensitivity to the fish's confusion or fear; I was chuckling because right then in that moment I felt part of it all—Yellowstone's autumn, the spawning run, the great seasonal migration which had pulled me all the way here from New Hampshire. Mission accomplished, I decided—those infamous words from our recent history. But it's the way I felt just then, and the truth is that in my time remaining in the park, though I fished just as hard as I had before, it was never with the same questing, semi-desperate intensity.

A few last words about this classic Yellowstone autumn weather. You're supposed to dress for it in layers, peeling off or adding on depending on what the conditions call for. This makes perfect sense, in theory, but when the autumn weather is as changeable as it is in Yellowstone—when a burst of sunlight raises the temperature ten degrees in three minutes, and a sudden cloud drops it back five degrees in two minutes—the effort involved in undressing and dressing is considerable.

In the morning, during a squall, I would be layered in silk liner socks, wool wading socks, long synthetic underwear bottoms, fleece pants, GORE-TEX waders, synthetic underwear tops, cotton turtleneck, down pullover, waterproof wading jacket, and orange ski cap. Layered with these, plus two chemical "heat packs" stuffed under my clothes against my waist, and a bourbon-laced tea in my thermos for restorative breaks on the bank. By ten, the most readily accessible of these layers had been taken off and stuffed in my fishing vest, but then by eleven, rain blowing back in again, most were back on, until noon, when the sun came out and I began sweating. After a few hours of this sort of alternation, one becomes convinced that the weather has a perverse sensitivity to what one is wearing, and tricks one accordingly—that it's not the weather influencing one's choice of clothing, but one's choice of clothing that influences the weather.

During the last few days of my trip things became much simpler, since, with the weather turning colder, a layer donned in the morning stayed on until I stripped for a shower that night. And snow was now a factor. When the cloud ceiling lifted off the mountains, the gray gave way to the most startling white imaginable. I had often seen snow on Yellowstone's summits, but always in July when it had been last winter's snow stubbornly hanging on—beautiful, in a grayish, wistful kind of way, but nothing as dramatic as I saw now. The summits were being layered in white so brilliant it made me squint even if the sun wasn't out, and streamers of the same color coated the gullies and ravines, emphasizing their rugged contours. The snow made the mountains seem both higher and more distant. Looking out toward the Gallatin Range, I could have been staring at the Himalayas. So high up was the snow, so immaculate and airy, that it didn't seem anything that could ever touch the valleys or affect my plans.

With the aspen still golden, the backdrop so perfect, it was tempting to think of a Yellowstone autumn as something static, the land posing for its perfect picture and giving you plenty of time to compose your shot. Autumn as something different, autumn as the precursor to brutal winter—well, this notion took a while to sink in. On one of my last days I drove along the Gallatin to fish Fan Creek, the lovely meadow stream along the western border of the park. There was no snow in West Yellowstone, but as soon as the highway crossed the height of land past Grayling Creek, the flakes started coming down fast and furious, and there was a dangerous coating on the road. Even in the car, I could sense the silence the snow imposed over the land—it was impossible to think that any noise could ever penetrate that smothering gray-ness—and I knew from many years in New England that once this silent, brooding snow arrives, you can kiss autumn goodbye.

Meanwhile, judging by phone calls home to my father and Celeste, record heat was the problem in the rest of the nation, with temperatures so high back in New Hampshire that my kids were still swimming in our local pond. Yellowstone seemed, in contrast, like a national park dedicated to preserving a primitive, unsullied slice of our original northern hemisphere climate, the one we've gotten used to over the past ten millennia. Just as visi-tors come to see remnant populations of wild bison or wolves in their natural setting, they might eventually come to the park for the nostalgic feeling of chilly fingers, or to show their kids what snowflakes on the tip of your tongue feels like, or how good standing in front of a crackling fire feels when you've spent all day out in the cold. *Visit Yellowstone!* tourism brochures of the future might say. *Experience the climate your grandparents once knew!*

Or not. As chilly as it was, I hadn't forgotten my first two weeks, the record high temperatures, constant sunshine and obvious drought. No artfully drawn borders, no careful management by ecologists, could prevent the climate changing in Yellowstone as it changed everywhere else. I had the disturbing feeling, both here and at home, that planet Earth had somehow skidded in its orbit and was now several hundred thousand miles closer to the sun than normal—that the absolutely perfect distance we owed life to, being neither too far from our star nor too close, was now a thing of the past. Or felt like it was. Equally disturbing, aside from what this new Age of Perspiration actually felt like on the skin, was the thought that humans had got their mitts on the climate—that we were players now when it came to weather, and ham-handed ones at that. We go to Yellowstone like we stare up at stars—to see a place unspoiled—and if we are messing up its weather, then soon there will be no reason to go at all.

A prediction no one else has bothered making yet: global warming will mean the end of nature writing of the old, lyrical, rapturous sort. How can a writer look upon nature now, even a small slice of it, without weeping? And, speaking of literature, let us now praise those angry and yet very shrewd Cassandras who have been warning us for two centuries that we were going to mess things up, from Henry David Thoreau to Henry Beston to Rachel Carson to Edward Abbey to Wendell Berry—they were right when the rest of us were wrong.

I remember in grade school, reading in our geography books, that old discredited theory about how stimulating our climate was in the mid-latitudes, just cold enough to breed an energetic race of eager go-getters, unlike in Africa where all was sloth. Intellectual rubbish, of course—but on the individual level, there was something to that. I had done very well with cold throughout my life. I loved the feel of warm mittens pulled on over cold fingers as a kid, or sledding on our unplowed streets after snow. I took up cross-country skiing when I was eighteen, before most people in this country had even heard of it. Snow, the way the light reflects off drifts, the impressionistic dots it leaves slanting across a border of pines, was something that had made it way into my writing often. When it came time to choose a home, a place to raise our family, we had gone as far north in New England as we could, and the first snowstorm outside our new home, settling against the foundation, had seemed like nature's seal of approval on our good fortune.

Even now, here in Yellowstone. The icy feel of the river through my waders. The way the wind cut and slashed at my clothes, but found no way past. The brilliance of the high snow, the silence of the snow lower down. The color cold brought to the aspens. If this was to be my last engagement with the climate that was ours for so many centuries, so be it—but I wasn't going to leave without trying my hand at writing its epitaph. America's was a temperate climate, which meant that sometimes we baked and sometimes we froze, but we had six good centuries to get used to it, and many of us liked it just fine.

Buffalo, if they wander outside the park's boundaries, are liable to be shot. They're said to carry a disease called brucellosis that

can spread to cattle and cause them to abort their calves—or at
least that's the justification put forth by ranchers. The solitary old
bulls that roam the park must have a highly developed sense of
where the boundaries are; one ranger told me that most of the
bison shot are younger males. Pushing the boundaries—fine,
that's what young bulls do—but respecting them is an admirable
trait, too, at least for a buffalo getting up there in years.

Once again, I found that I could easily identify with them. During my three weeks at Yellowstone I became reluctant to leave
the park for even a single afternoon—felt that if I did so the
spell would be broken. There's a take-out hamburger stand in
Gardiner, five minutes from the north entrance: Helen's Corral,
a favorite of mine from way back when. I drove there from Mammoth the last night in the season they were open, treated myself
to a buffalo burger (so much for that fellow feeling), and felt, all
the time I was there, as exposed and vulnerable as one of those
park-straying bison.

Toward the end of my trip, I ventured west of the park to fish
the Madison River below Hebgen, meeting my good friend Tom
Ciardelli there, who was celebrating his fifty-fifth birthday with a
trip of his own. The Madison is fabled trout water, and while I've
fished it a number of times over the years, its challenges don't
quite match my fishing style. It's a constant series of riffles and
rapids, the water seems intoxicated by its own speed and dash, but
I'm the kind of guy who likes an occasional piece of slack water
or an actual pool. Still, I had fun the afternoon we spent there.
The aspens along Hebgen Lake were the most brilliant I saw on
the entire trip, and I managed to catch some small-but-insouciant
trout on tiny Serendipity nymphs—and lost two that, had I landed
them, would have been the subject of two bragging paragraphs

here. Driving back toward the park at dusk, I had that distant view of it I particularly love, and which can only be obtained from the west looking in toward the high plateau extending south from the Gallatins. A lost world where anything could happen, that's what it looks like under an autumn sunset . . . and since it *is* a lost world where anything can happen, I don't have to worry about my simile being far-fetched.

I stayed in West Yellowstone's cheapest motel that night, the only night I wasn't ensconced within the park's boundaries. And while there's a raffish, unapologetic charm about West Yellowstone that I've always enjoyed—especially in autumn, when the streets, shops and restaurants are quiet, even lonely—I became anxious to tuck myself back within the park before the ranchers shot me for brucellosis.

The truth is that my little excursion to West Yellowstone was a turning point. On every trip a point is reached where you realize that you've gone as far as you're going to go this time. Geographically, yes, but often emotionally as well—the two often coinciding, your furthest north, east, west or south matching your deepest imaginative release. That point passed, your thoughts begin wandering from intoxicating concentration on the here and now to the problems and challenges awaiting you at home. A seesaw, a teeter-totter—there's never been a trip when I couldn't mark the precise moment when the trip became less about going and more about returning home. The precise moment for me on this trip was an early evening dinner at one of the cafes on Madison Street, when, finishing my chicken steak smothered in too much gravy, writing up the wonders of the day in my notebook, I found myself jotting down reminders of chores and obligations awaiting me at home.

My worry of all worries was the state of my father's health. Frankly, in putting together this account, I thought that when it came time to write of my father it would be a loving elegy. Almost a year ago he was diagnosed with a rare blood disease, one whose denouement usually comes within six months. But Dad is still going strong, getting close now to his eighty-seventh birthday, in a new home, with new friends, in a new town. This is surprising, at least in one sense. Dad has never been someone you'd describe as hard, tough or feisty, and yet it's become clear now that we've always underestimated this side of him, overlooked an inner strength that has enabled him to survive challenges that would have long ago polished off a lesser man.

Dad's still going strong—but I worry about him even more than I worry about my kids, which means I'm a member of the sandwich generation, a gentle term for the vise many people my age feel squeezed in. In an earlier era, children were out on their own by the time they were seventeen or eighteen, and parents were often gone before they reached sixty-five, so the years that middle-aged people had to be concerned about caring for both their kids and their parents were very few. That's all changing now. Children need support at least through their college years, and often for some time after; parents are living to a riper old age, so there may be twenty-five years now where middle-aged adults have to use their strength and resources to help out both generations, with all kinds of conflicting tugs pulling them now toward one, now toward the other.

Sandwich generation. I had heard the term, but had never absorbed the full force of it, not until a morning eight years ago when between one moment and the next the vise not only gripped me in its jaws, it all but crushed me.

It was just after dawn on a wretchedly gray day in early winter. Celeste had already left for work. The phone rang—and I rolled across the bed to pick it up. It was Dad. My father, though—and this is what terrified me—seemed *not* my father, so strange was his voice and tone. He babbled on about something incomprehensible, money, the safety deposit box, how we were all going to starve, then the words ran away from him and he started crying, crying desperately. "Dad, listen," I said, under the illusion that my calmness would pull him together. "Deep breath, Dad"—but my voice couldn't find a way around his sobs.

I had no idea what to do, how to react. Never had I become so terrified and helpless so suddenly. Then, as my father sobbed, Matthew ran in from downstairs. He was crying too, and it had nothing to do with my father's call. As he threw himself down on the bed beside me and grabbed me, I heard his cries in one ear, and in the other ear my father's.

I remember thinking, in the one moment of lucidity I managed, that this was pain in stereo, the vise closing, the sandwich generation defined.

Who to comfort first? Matt lay next to me, I could put my arm around him and pull him closer, but what to do about my father three hundred miles away? I don't remember what I said or did to quiet both of them—the horrid details have been seared from my memory. My father, having coped so bravely with my mother's illness and death a year before, had now collapsed from loneliness and strain. Matt, when we rushed him to the pediatrician's office, was diagnosed as suffering an intestinal virus and given a prescription.

And then things got worse.

We brought my father to New Hampshire, tried to snap him

out of it with plain old-fashioned TLC, but it soon became apparent that we were up against something none of us had any experience with—a full-fledged depressive "episode" that eventually required hospitalization. And Matthew's stomachache did not go away, despite another visit to the doctor. In having to decide which one to focus most of my energy and concern on that winter, I chose my father—which turned out to be a life-threatening mistake. Three months later, after Matthew's stomachache had returned several more times, he collapsed; we rushed him to the hospital for emergency surgery on a ruptured appendix—surgery that, if I hadn't been so concerned with nursing my father through his crisis, might have been done much earlier, in more routine conditions.

Having to choose between my father and my son—and this wasn't just a metaphorical choice, but one that involved many day-to-day decisions—I had picked wrong, and the guilt of this, the rue, clouds my relationship with my father to this day. He snapped out of it eventually, thanks to antidepressants and some aggressive therapy; he proved again how surprisingly tough he is in his inner core. But those three months of crisis changed something essential in our relationship. I find—and the guilt is very heavy—that in talking with him on the phone, in going to visit, in helping him cope with the changes in his life and the weight of his years, there has arisen a new limit of involvement that I won't let myself cross. I feel empathy for him, pity, but—and I'm being brutally honest here—I can't help feeling that at some fundamental level that pity poses a threat. That in apportioning out my emotions, my energy, my attention, I can never make the same mistake that I made eight years ago, and which, if things had turned out just a little differently, might have cost me my son.

Dad needs me. My son needs me. I can't always be there for both of them, but I'll always be there for my son.

Again, this makes me feel guilty. Here I am, in temporary command of the family lifeboat, ready to kick my father overboard to make room for my son. If you draw back and take the larger view, it's probably the natural and healthy response, biologically speaking. If our emotions have to choose between our parents and our kids—and life is not shy about presenting us with this choice, in all kinds of ways—we have to pick our kids every time. Sometimes we pick harshly. Other times we find ways to soften it. Never is the balance quite right.

The essayist Dan Jacobson has a good analysis of the resulting conundrum. Why, if our parents become like children, can't we cherish them like we do our kids. "Just as the parents of young children feel bound to protect and help them, to shield them from the ugliness of life and its dangers," he writes, "so grown children begin to feel that they have this obligation toward their parents. Indeed, if parents live long enough and suffer the illnesses and deprivations which age inevitably brings, they will revert to being children, wrinkled children, impossible children; beings whom their children will care for out of affection, out of pity, out of piety, out of exasperation, out of regard for the past, hardly out of passion."

Fair enough—but there's a brutal side to this, too. "Children are loveable, and are loved, precisely and to the degree that they are vulnerable," Jacobson writes. "If we were not moved to cherish them by such manifestations of weakness, the race would not survive. The vulnerability of old people, on the other hand, has no such appeal; they've exhausted their usefulness, racially speaking, and nature has no compunction in making this face as evident to everyone around them as it makes obvious the charm and vitality of children."

That's the problem in a nutshell, one that doesn't play out on an evolutionary scale or philosophically, but in day-to-day family decisions that are often wrenching. What Jacobson doesn't mention, and what many people forget, is that the sandwich-generation dilemma doesn't just come from having children younger than us to care for, and, yes, "children" older than us. We late-middle-aged are still partly children ourselves, in so many ways, needing approbation, sympathy, advice and comfort as much as we ever have—and not to be able to count on this can be frightening. Our children look to us for help, our parents look to us for help—but if they only knew how much help we need ourselves! We will row, bail, plug the leaks, do the best we can for as long as need to do it—and yet how often we'd like to send up distress flares, fire rockets, have the Coast Guard come rescue *us*.

My father was born in 1917, which means that he turned fifty-five in 1972. He wore his late middle age lightly, judging by the picture of him behind me on the bookcase, the one where he's hugging my mother and beaming from ear to ear at a surprise party my sister and I threw for their anniversary that summer. He still has a fine shock of blond, wavy hair; his features are self-evidently those of a friendly, decent man; his baby-faced, All-American-boy quality is still discernible. He was fit, though he didn't exercise other than walking; he never smoked, never ate too much, and while he enjoyed a beer at his monthly poker game, it was seldom more than one or two.

In his life there was much to be thankful for, some solid accomplishments. His career continued to go well. He sold insurance and was extraordinarily good at it; since he was so obviously honest, and delivered his sales pitch with such sincerity and directness, it was hard for people to say no; he had just been selected as a charter member of the Liberty Mutual Hall of Fame. Money was not a problem; he was prudent with it, but the mere acquisition of riches for their own sake interested him not at all. His wife, my mother, he adored. His daughter was grown up now, a kindergarten teacher about to marry a very good man. His son? Well, that was more complicated, he kept dropping out of college, quitting his various jobs, said he wanted to be a writer, whatever *that* meant. But he wasn't into drugs or drinking or anything a father need be ashamed about, and the family ties were still very close, very affectionate.

Besides this? He still talked with a slight Brooklyn accent, though four years at Lehigh and a stint in the army softened most of it ("oil" was almost but not quite pronounced "earl"). He liked to play golf, though considering his eyesight, a strange kind of golf. He liked telling mildly off-color jokes. He went to church on Sunday without being particularly passionate about it—his religion was the sentimental, nostalgic kind that had never really matured past Sunday school. If his religious, political and ethical beliefs weren't very strong one way or the other, at least he wasn't the kind to foist his morals on anyone else; live and let live was his philosophy, though unlike my mother he never used aphorisms to sum things up. He believed in staying away from trouble, which meant staying away from the troubled; he drew his friends not from the quietly desperate but from the quietly content. (One generational fact strikes me with great force: my parents knew not one couple that was divorced; Celeste and I would have to think for a while before we came up with friends who *hadn't* been divorced.)

He was a good man more because of what he *wasn't* rather than what he was. Living in a snobby town, he didn't have a stuck-up gene in his body. Status meant nothing to him, he wasn't even aware of it as a concept. Macho? His poor eyesight, his inability to perform typical male chores like carpentry, meant that he helped Mom instead with the dishes, swept, took a hand's-on approach to child raising, a New Age dad far ahead of his time. Greedy? Milkshakes and neckties were his only extravagances. Conformity or non-conformity hardly applied to him; if he lived what was in many ways the typical suburban life, he did it because it matched his tastes, not because its tastes molded him. His emotions, his interests, were all caught up with his work, home and family; whenever the outside world caught his attention he was genuinely interested, but the outside world hardly ever caught his attention anymore, and this was one of the danger signs that might have been apparent if anyone had bothered analyzing him at fifty-five—that his world, as comfortable as it was for him, was relatively narrow and sheltered. His personal growth had largely stopped, and his nostalgia, his sentimentality, made him increasingly vulnerable to the buffets of change.

The odd and unexpected traits in him—and these were many—were all connected to problems with his eyes. He had experienced trouble during the war; in his army scrapbook, along with patches and postcards, were formal reprimands from commanding officers berating him for crashing yet another jeep—accidents caused by his increasing myopia. On the day I was born he was in a hospital having his tonsils removed, since some quack ascribed his dimming vision to tonsillitis. In truth, he was suffering from macular degeneration—common among old people, but extremely rare in people in their thirties. As long as I could remember, he had been "legally blind." He read newspapers so close to his eyes that his nose became smudged with newsprint. He listened to talking books supplied by the Library of Congress. He bumped into furniture, and his arms and legs were often black and blue.

He didn't drive, hadn't for twenty-five years, other than to back the car out of the garage. He could hardly sign his name to any paperwork. His insurance success came totally from his talent on the telephone. When he played golf, he could see just well enough to focus on a hazy ball on a hazier tee, but he had no idea where the ball went after he hit it, and his buddies would have to lead him to his next shot.

How hard this was for him, how terrifying, it's difficult to judge, since he seldom talked about it. In all the time I've known him, he's never once complained about his eyesight, not *once*. Jokes? Yes, a lot of jokes told on himself, with wry laughter. Walking off the boat dock at our summer place in his business suit; throwing out my mother's favorite jewelry thinking it was that morning's trash; having long conversations with "friends" who turned out to be strangers . . . no one ever tells a story on himself with as much good humor as Dad.

But if he met his handicap with tremendous courage, patience and humor, there was a price to be paid, and, at fifty-five, the nature of this price was just starting to become apparent. Dad had a talent for telling white lies, which came not only from a fertile, underemployed imagination, but from the various excuses he had made up over the years to compensate for being almost blind. Dad didn't look blind, and he could see just well enough to get himself into trouble. People—clerks at the post office, tellers at the bank—would shove something at him to be signed, and rather than admitting that he couldn't see, he would make up a story about not being able to read (which must have seemed less embarrassing to him than the truth). His white lies had become so chronic that they became laughable—ordering Chinese food from a takeout restaurant, he would leave his name as "Hale" rather than "Wetherell"—and, at fifty-five, the truth was becoming so elastic in small matters, that it made me wonder if the truth in larger matters might not start to run away from him, too.

Handicapped, he couldn't indulge himself in any hobbies, and he had no real avocation to turn to for amusement or solace. How much he would have benefited from being able to model airplanes or collect stamps. Underutilized, his intelligence was vulnerable, and into the vacuum rushed what was already a world-class talent for worrying.

And worrying led to insomnia. He paced the hall a lot at night, spent many restless hours tossing and turning, and often, by afternoon of the next day, could hardly stay awake. (He reminded me later of old Prince Bolkonski in *War and Peace*, unable to sleep, ordering his servants to move his bed from room to room, never able to separate himself form his demons.) He had gone to a "sleep-wake" clinic, been wired with electrodes, but aside from changing his sleeping pill prescriptions, the doctors hadn't come up with an answer.

"Stop worrying!" is what they told him. It's what we all told him. *Stop worrying, Dad. Dad, you worry too much. Dad, why not ease off on the worrying?* Such were the feeble, puny darts we tossed at his depression—a clinical depression that was so well camouflaged by his genial good humor, a depression so much darker and more mysterious than any of us could fathom, that for many vital years nothing was done to head it off.

Dad worried about his health, his heart, his kids, and yet he never once worried about the thing he should have worried about most—worry itself, what it was doing to him, how it was slowing nibbling away at his geniality, courage and optimism, a battle waged out of sight of any of us, out of sight probably even to him. This was what finally burst upon us on that terrible morning when I received his desperate, sobbing phone call—but that was still twenty-five years in the future, and the incremental steps that led up to it, bizarre as some of these were, we all put down to Dad just being Dad.

And just as I can't describe his happiness without mentioning this new and ominous cloud, I can't describe the cloud without saying that for the most part Dad at fifty-five was absolutely at his peak—a funny, good-humored man whose complete lack of vanity and pretense made him a delight to be around. What's more, he had that Greatest Generation kind of fox-trotting, jitterbugging bounce and drive, the satisfaction of having survived the Depression, survived the war, come into riches beyond which any of his generation ever dreamed of—perhaps the happiest example of postponed gratification in the history of the world. There was a lot of this in Dad. A house in the suburbs. A new car every five years. A vacation cottage on a New England lake. Good schools for his kids. To a man who remembered crowded, cold-water walk-ups in Brooklyn, it was heaven.

If I could go back in time and give him some late-middle-age advice, it might be to try to distance himself from his life for a while, to try to see it from a new angle, take stock, regroup—but that's silly of me, he was simply never the kind of man to regard his life this way. Don't worry, Dad, is what I would end up telling him. Don't ask me how, but I can see thirty years into the future, and I know that most of your worries will come to nothing. You're not going to die prematurely of a heart attack, your son is not going to starve in the gutter, your eyesight is not going to get any worse, your insomnia is not going to kill you. Don't worry, dad. Don't worry about a bloody thing.

"Dad, don't worry about small things anymore, promise me that?"

"Oh, I won't, I won't! You're absolutely right, Walter. From now on I'm just going to take life as it comes. This talk has done me a world of good."

Last winter in his kitchen, me trying to convince him that it is time to give up the house and move to assisted living. We sit across from each other at the kitchen table, Dad leaning slightly sideways in his chair, his right leg crossed over his left knee, me sitting slightly sideways in my chair, my right leg crossed over my left knee—so genetically similar that our very joints are aligned, find comfort in the same positions.

Age hasn't been particularly kind to his face, but it hasn't been brutal either. His eyes, weak as they are, are clear, not rheumy. His hair still has traces of blond in it. His disarming smile, always his strong suit, has become tentative; he often smiles carefully now, gingerly, as if it might hurt.

The table in front of us is covered with a blizzard of white paper. He writes notes to himself in black marker large enough for his myopia to decipher—reminders, exhortations, admonitions. Call this doctor or that. Take pills. Empty trash. Concentrate on one day at a time

ONE DAY AT A TIME! There are so many of these that he has to write reminders to find reminders, but these get forgotten, too, and I have no compunction, when he leaves to answer the telephone, in sweeping them with the side of my hand into the trash.

"Telemarketers," he says, shaking his head. "What do they want with me?"

"The house looks good, Dad," I say, edging slowly into my pitch. "You're doing a great job."

He smiles, ruefully. "I try, Walter."

"But you know, it's getting to be a lot for any one man to handle. I see the refrigerator is going. The roof looks like monsters have been chewing on it. The siding needs washing. There's a lot of heavy maintenance I don't think anyone your age should be asked to take on."

Aside from these, though I don't mention it to him, the house smells. Smells of old M&Ms fallen into cracks by the stove, liniment oozing out of its tube, general mustiness, iodine, wet towels. Though I ticked off my list of things that needed replacing or repairing, it is this smell more than anything that convinces me that after fifty years of living there, the house has become too much for him and that it is time to move on.

"Dad, look. You're legally blind. You've fallen down a few times now; all your old friends are either gone or moved away, so you have no support system anymore. The neighbors are all young. It's different times now, let's face it; they don't care for anyone but themselves. I'm up in New Hampshire. Christina works her hardest, but she can't do it all for you. You'll be happy out there. It will be like the old neighborhood in Brooklyn, lots of people, new friends."

He takes that in, in silence—he seems to be trying to convince himself that it's true. "Well, when I was on that last visit, I didn't see anyone. That's what gets me. You never see anyone out in the halls."

"It's not a cruise ship, Dad. People are in their apartments relaxing. You'll see them at dinner or when you go to the pool."

"Emptying the house out would be one hell of a job." He waves his arm around; the accumulated bric-a-brac—my mother's ancient African violets, furniture, pots and pans, clothing seems (he's always been good at drawing me into his perspective) overwhelming, anchors that could never be pulled from the kelp. "One hell of a job."

"Christina and I will help you. We'll all pitch in. It will be easier than you think."

The conversation is not going the way I want. The way I want it to go is the way I wanted all my conversations with my father to go ever since I was thirteen: to have him be swayed by the utter rightness of my logic and give in.

A couple of factors worked against this. Everything I say, to my ears, sounds scripted and rehearsed, like I'm reading my lines off a teleprompter. *Where does this come from?* I wonder—and then realize that it's because my exact words are almost certainly being delivered in much the same tone all over the country at the same time, as thousands of people born in 1948 sit in their parents' kitchens trying to convince people born in 1917 what the sensible and prudent thing would be for them to do.

While I know intellectually that Dad is old now, my emotions don't really buy into this. For me—despite the bruised, helpless skin, the tremble in his hands, the memory that slips and slides over things that happened just the day before—Dad isn't old at all. We bear the same mathematical relationship to each other that we always have; he is, as he's always been, thirty-two years older than me. If I looked at him through the eyes of a twenty-year-old, he would appear ancient, but I'm looking at him through the eyes of a fifty-four-year-old, and, to a fifty-four-year-old he looks remarkably boyish still, the same young Dad I've always known.

And one more problem to confuse things further. Though I talk reasonably, while I try to bring all my accumulated wisdom, maturity and sense to the issue, I realize that these mean nothing to my father—that when it comes to our ages, the same hocus-pocus is influencing his point of view. He isn't talking to a mature, experienced, late-middle-age man who has learned a lot from life, or a novelist who understands a bit about the human condition. He is talking to someone who, in his eyes, is still only seven. Why, in that case, take me seriously?

"Yep," he says, closing his eyes. "Fifty years of stuff. One hell of a job cleaning it out."

"Dad, I'm no spring chicken myself now."

"You don't see anyone walking around in the halls, that's what gets me. A bunch of old people, that's it."

One piece of scrap paper I've missed. I reach over for it, pick it up to read the smudged black ink. *In case of death contact my son Walter D. Wetherell or my daughter Christina Lane.* And with that, something snaps in me, I mutter something about having to call home, get up, walk quickly from the kitchen in the general direction of my old room.

My father had turned it into a kind of study, though most of the furniture there had been there when I was little. My old dresser. My old bookcase. My old chair—crippled-looking, arthritic, torn, defenseless. None of this makes me feel nostalgic, though it would have if I had let it; that's what I'm doing on this visit, ruthlessly choking back all the nostalgia, as if to prove that if I can do it then so can Dad. There are a lot of appeals in that room—the past tugs hard—but I ignore them and scan the various boxes and trunks with the cold, hard eye of a professional mover. Cartons of old slides that no one would ever look at again, shoeboxes with army patches from the war, bundles of old Perry Como records and Mitch Miller. I look at these, deciding what could be thrown out and what needs to be saved. One hell of a job? My father was right about that. It would take a person of brutal insensitivity to do it right.

The largest box, the only one I examine closely, contains, among other pictures, an unframed photo I had seen before, but not in years. It's a photo of my father somewhere in England during the war, posing with some fellow officers leaning back against a jeep, all three looking half-drunk and giddy, not so much on alcohol as on the sheer pleasure of being young, handsome, and alive. They wear Eisenhower jackets, officers' flat hats. Dad is movie-star handsome, his hair—even in black and white—a happy sweep of blond. On his face is a cockiness that I wouldn't have associated with him, but it's a smart, alert cockiness, without any trace of vanity or ego. He's a man who fits comfortably into his world in a way he never quite managed in all the long years after. He has no worries; something larger absorbs them, blots them out. This young man, much younger than me, is so appealing, innocent, and happy that I want to embrace and cherish him in a way—though I hated myself for this—that I could never embrace the man who was waiting for me back in the kitchen.

And that brings tears to my eyes. Time stopped. Time regained. Time sitting in my hands, the past and present simultaneously, and yet I don't know what on earth to do with it, so, like the old papers in my father's study, it becomes just another thing to throw away.

I go back to the kitchen. Dad is down on his hands and knees fussing with the radiator, trying to bleed it so it will work. He curses, bangs with his hand, puts his face up close to the valve, trying to see.

"Careful, Dad," I say, too softly for him to hear.

He is the same boy as in the photo; there is no real difference other than the illusory one of his looks. The wrinkles. The black-and-blue splotches. The sparse hair. None of these matter; I'm looking past them to a twenty-seven-year-old man in the springtime of his life, second-in-command of a camp for German POWs in rural Wiltshire, circa 1944, me a pipsqueak kid who knows nothing about life compared to him. And just because I am still a pipsqueak, I make my voice go as harsh and brutal as it can go.

"Dad, get up, don't fuss with that now."

"It's not working."

"Dad, you're moving, simple as that. We can't take care of you here anymore, and you can't take care of yourself."

Dad boosts himself stiffly back into his chair, exhausted by the effort. He turns to face me, or where he thinks I am. "I know that," he says softly.

"It's not a question of your happiness anymore, whether you'll be bored out there or not. It's a question of safety."

"When spring comes," he says, not quite managing to make it a question.

"No, Dad. Now."

He stares down at his hands, turns to the window, tries making out the old crab apple tree that has shaded the porch for so many years.

"I love you, Walter."

It's something he learned to say after his breakdown—something

we all learned to say, after fifty years of not knowing well enough
how.

"We love you, Dad. Everything will turn out for the best; trust
us, you'll see."

That was ten months ago. Dad now lives on the North Fork of
Long Island, in a retirement community, an assisted living facility
that is one of thousands popping up all over the country to take
care of an aging population. It's a well-run, attractively designed
place; this first round of residents are those of the Greatest Generation who bought their suburban homes for almost nothing
back in the fifties, then sold them for fantastic amounts as the
century came to an end—enough to spend the last years of their
lives in relative luxury. Dad has made friends, since many of
them share the same background—brought up in Brooklyn or
Queens or the Bronx, back when no one had a dime, serving in
the war, working hard and long for good corporations, retiring
with generous pensions and their health. Eating together on the
patio overlooking the Sound, sitting around the pool gabbing,
helping each other—like new kids in high school—find their
way around the halls. There are a lot of memories to share, they
like to trade jokes with each other, and this all seems very much
like a happy ending.

It hasn't been perfect, of course. Waking up one night in his
new bedroom, unsure of where he was, Dad tripped and fell,
resulting in a bump on his head that required surgery. (So much
for safety.) A real scare, bad enough that it could have finished
off a weaker, less spirited man, but Dad's recovered and is back
in his apartment now, back on his feet.

Celeste, Erin, Matthew, and I visited this summer, taking the
ferry over from New London. Dad took us around, showing off

the amenities; he kept raving the whole time about how polite and friendly everyone was. We swam in the pool with him. We took him out for ice cream. He held my arm a lot more than he ever has before, and if it was partly for support, it was also because he needed to keep contact, needed to touch me as badly as he needed to touch me when I was a little boy. He'd have to let go soon. Yes, we both understood that, it colors every minute we have now. But that moment wasn't yet.

A lot of people stopped us in the hall, said hello to my father, said "This must be your son!" Dad beamed, while I inwardly cringed, just like I cringed when I was eleven and people said that. I could never see the resemblance myself—but I can see it now, if I look in a mirror and don't blink.

We went back to Dad's apartment and talked. I was disappointed to find that though life was so much better for him here, he still worried about things as much as always. My sister and I had arranged for my niece to live in his old house temporarily, and he had all kinds of concerns about that. I tried reassuring him, felt my irritation growing the more he went on.

Why couldn't he be serene now, happy? Why couldn't he outlive his worries the way some people seem to outlive old age, entering a tranquil postlude where the petty concerns of the world drop away and finally they're content to just merely be? Why, for that matter, couldn't a son stop wanting his father to be perfect? Maybe I was wrong about his worrying; maybe worrying was Dad's hobby, the only pursuit absorbing enough to have ever fully engaged his first-class mind—Dad's version of fly-fishing. Maybe worrying had kept him going this long, past World War One; past Hitler, Stalin and Nixon; past the Depression, World War Two, the Cold War, Vietnam; past the Spanish Flu, the polio epidemic, the invention of television and computers; past the Soviet Union, which had been born the same year he had, but had died fifteen years earlier; past all these things. Who was I to take away his hobby now?

"Dad," I said, when he had gone over all the details that troubled him. "Please don't worry."

"Oh, I won't, I won't!" he vowed. Then, two minutes later: "Does Kristin know how to bleed the radiators?"

The important thing is that he seems to like it where he is, and has help if he needs help. I'm proud that he's able to try on a new life after eighty-seven years, proud that he can still find the initiative and energy to round up new poker buddies. It's a cliché, this business about our parents sheltering us from death, but it's true, and I'm not looking forward to having that shelter disappear (just as I'm not looking forward to having what seems the even more protective shelter of child raising disappear when Celeste and I become empty nesters).

But maybe I'm wrong about this, just as I seem to be wrong about so much in my relationship with my father. Maybe, having gone before us (to use that peaceful old phrase), your parents still shelter you when they're deceased. You gulp when they leave, and you step forward until you're at the head of the queue waiting to go next; you know that the ones you love have crossed the border already, and so, in a last gesture of comfort, they extend their hands and help you cross, too. "I think about Mom and Dad a lot now," Dad said, there toward the end of our visit. That's all he said—but I'm old enough now that I know what he meant.

All in all, a good visit. "Your visit has done me good!" Dad kept saying, and just before we left, Celeste gathered us for pictures out on the lawn in front of his apartment, Grandpop on one side,

me in the middle, the two kids on the other side. "Move closer!"
Celeste kept saying as we hugged to fit the frame. "Closer!" We
tried moving even tighter, put our arms around each other and
squeezed, and against all the forces of separation that pried at us,
we finally managed it just as the flashbulb went off, we three generations of Wetherells pressed as tightly together as it's humanly
possible to be.

The actual day of my birthday, the big 5–5, I spent fishing Muleshoe
Bend on the Firehole River. If you've ever driven from Madison
Junction toward Old Faithful, you've passed it on the right, shortly
beyond the Midway Geyser Basin. The river has been in sight,
boiling or seeming to boil, and then suddenly the bank swells into
a small hill, and you lose sight of the water for several seconds.
Where it comes back into view—and you've had to crane your
head around to see it properly—is the section of river known to
fly-fishers as Muleshoe Bend. (Charlie Brooks, an old-time fishing
writer, took credit for naming it; there are many such nicknames
for the park's river bends and pools, names that have endeared
themselves to anglers over the years, but appear on no map.) Up
against a ridge on the far left you can just make out the top of an
old iron bridge; below the bridge, the river unfolds in a pronounced
curve that almost doubles back on itself. The hill by the road slants
down to this in a wide gully, and, widening further, serves as the
wall of a shallow amphitheater, at the bottom of which sits the
finest stretch to fish.

   Me, if I had been a legendary old-time fishing writer, I'd have
named it "Horseshoe Bend," but I'm guessing, though I don't
know for sure, that a mule's shoe is wider and a bit more open
than a horse's. Actually, I would have named it "Fly Loop Bend,"

since that's what the sinuous curve reminds me of: the open loop
a fly line describes in the air when it's cast by a vintage bamboo
fly rod. (Look at the angling watercolors of Winslow Homer, and
you'll see him trace that curve over and over again.)

I had fished Muleshoe twice this trip, and, on my birthday—with
a good twenty rivers to choose from—it was the one spot I had to
fish again. To say that it's the most beautiful four hundred yards of
trout stream I know would not be an exaggeration, though—this
being Yellowstone—it's an otherworldly kind of beauty that might
not be to everyone's taste. The Firehole is the river that Old Faithful's waters runs into, as well as those of hundreds of other geysers
and hot springs, so it's a miracle that it even holds trout at all. It
does, and in great numbers, though perhaps not as big as they
were forty yeas ago, when the river wasn't quite as warm as it's
become since (due, it's thought, to seismic activity and global
warming). The trout have a reputation for extreme wariness, are
wonderfully discriminating when deciding which of the abundant
insects hatching on the surface they will deign to devour, and
catching even a small one can often take extraordinary delicacy
and patience.

That said, they were something of an excuse for me, these over-
educated rainbows and browns—they served as the magnets that
pulled me out of the car down to the river's banks where I could
drink in as much beauty as my inadequate soul could handle.
The river itself isn't much wider than a good cast, say sixty or
seventy feet across, and it's shallow enough that the weeds on
the bottom, flowing like a girl's hair downstream, give a striated
quality to the water, though the green is lightened considerably
by the lava comprising the streambed proper. (And the weed isn't
a marshy, oleaginous weed—it's as fine and fresh as watercress.)

Toward the middle of the stretch, on the slightest of rises thirty feet in from the bank, is a round patch of watery, yellow-white soil that bleeds a trickle of extraordinarily hot water down the lip of the bank into the river. A hot spring? A paint pot? One of the remarkable things about Yellowstone's thermal features is that many of them are so odd in their variations that it's impossible to definitively label them one thing or the other.

Directly across the river, the valley widens considerably, giving an expansive view, not only of the embracing ridge to the west, but the open basin of Midway to the north, punctuated by exclamation marks of steam. In the sunlight, this gives an extraordinary effect, a land of golden sage and shrub smoking in silver mist; and, if you wait for sunset, the vapor then takes on a wistful, lonely kind of color that is beyond my powers to describe. Closer, on the east side of the river, the bank steepens into a cliff, nudging the river out into its final curve—a curve topped by a geyser, an unnamed one that went off about every forty minutes with a whale-like spouting noise that never failed to startle me, no matter how many times in the course of the day I heard it. Later in the morning I fished down to it. It was exactly as if a hot tub, the kind big enough to seat six, had been sunk into the side of the bank. As I watched, someone hiding in the bushes turned a switch to make it bubble and churn—surely, there could be no other explanation—but some malfunction, some sudden surge of power, made it suddenly boil upward and overflow, all but somersaulting me over in my haste to back off.

An anonymous geyser. Land that bubbles. A river that steams. Any one of these wonders would have warranted inclusion in its own separate national park, but here in Yellowstone it's just part of the background, run-of-the-mill enchantment. I took my fill of it, though. For long minutes I lay stretched out on the crusty lava near the patch of land that cooked—staring, soaking up the view, trying as writers do to form words into a lasso with which I could rope things in. I hadn't forgotten my resolution about wonder I'd made back at the lake, and though my immersion in it wasn't perfect, the scene was so glorious that even the distractions it offered only deepened the wonders, made me concentrate all the more on the here and now.

Rising trout were the distractions. There right in front of me, not three feet from where the superheated water entered the river, a small brown was tipping up to take flies from the surface. Farther out, slightly larger trout rose time and time again, with exuberant, splashy sips, and there along the grassy far bank—tucked in tight to its under-curled, mustached lip—were slower, deeper risers, almost certainly fifteen- or sixteen-inch fish.

The rises stopped when I waded into the river, but once my ripples subsided, the fish began feeding again—if anything, even more exuberantly than before. Fly-fishers will be interested to know what they were taking, but the truth is that I couldn't quite puzzle this out. There were little Baetis mayflies on the water, but midges as well, and some squished-looking spinners, and even some meaty-looking white caddis flies. I tried flies that imitated all of these, and now and then would catch a fish, usually when I changed and offered them something different, but without ever feeling I had solved the mystery of what they especially preferred.

Fishing these Firehole trout as they rose all about me was very close to my happiest moment of my entire stay. From a fishing point of view, this was all about the concentration and smarts it took to persuade one of those trout that my fly was real, the soul-relaxing tension—fly-fishers will understand what I mean—where nothing, not even universe-class scenery or bugling elk, can distract you from your mission. Those who don't fish can perhaps think of it this way: what a thrill it would be to stand in the midst of from thirty to forty feeding wild animals who are not alarmed at your presence, but who, as it were, admit you as one of their number, so—much to your surprise and pleasure—you are suddenly an honorary elk, antelope, or water ouzel; their wildness embraces you, strips you of your noisy, smelly human shell, immersing you in nature in a way far beyond anything you ever dreamed of. That's what fishing to those rising Firehole trout was like—an initiation ceremony much more lavish and satisfying than anything I deserved.

The trout I caught weren't big, not the ones I took on the surface, but I've never been a size snob, and a ten-inch Firehole brown is a worthy and wondrous thing. As the day wore on, in the spirit of experimentation, I walked upstream to the iron bridge, then fished back down to my base camp using a sink-tip line and a black Wooly Bugger. This resulted in some bigger fish, two or three of fifteen inches, and a great many missed strikes. They were coming short to the Bugger, so I took my clippers and cut off the little tail on the end, transforming it from a Wooly Bugger, the champion streamer of today, to a Wooly Worm, the ex-champ from an earlier era.

There was another ingredient in my happiness: I fished that day with my birthday present, a brand-new Winston fly rod. Through a superhuman effort of self-control, I had carried it in my luggage throughout my stay without taking it out of its case—not until now, the big day, when I had a river and trout worthy of its debut. The great thing about this rod, so the ad copy said, was its combination of power at a distance and delicacy up close—and, surprisingly, this wasn't hyperbole, but an accurate description of its unique capabilities. It loaded quickly—meaning that almost immediately into each cast I could feel its flex start working—and yet, when I reached for the far bank, it was without any feeling of strain. I willed my fly to land in a certain place, and the rod delivered the fly right on target.

I could rhapsodize more here, but—well, this is far enough. In a lifetime devoted to *not* collecting anything, a good fly rod is the one thing I'm a sucker for, and the reason for this is that's it's the one and only tool I've ever learned to wield properly, the one and only instrument I've ever learned to play in tune, the one brush I've ever wielded with satisfying results.

By the time morning turned toward afternoon, I had worked out a good routine. Cast for trout, lie on bank, soak in scenery, walk downstream, sit, eat an apple, gaze, drink some tea, wade, cast. My downstream ramble led me once again to the unnamed geyser, and I stared into it like Narcissus into his pool, hoping I had the timing right and that my eyes wouldn't be scalded.

Did I see myself reflected there? I did not. I saw instead a bulbous bubble of opaque stream. But not a *lifeless* bubble. Diverse life forms find that water heated to 162 degrees Fahrenheit is exactly what they need to thrive—bacteria that stain the water green and yellow, but otherwise remain invisible, the life form in Yellowstone that's constructed the best defenses, adopted the best disguise. (In 1965 a microbiologist discovered a bacterium in the Mushroom Pool of the Lower Geyser Basin; known as "Taq," it produces an enzyme known as "Taq polymerase," which, with its usefulness in gene-replicating procedures, has come to be called the "Swiss army knife of molecular biology.") A silvery rock with a beautiful name, "geyserite," often surrounds a hot

spring's center, and I wondered if that was what I was experiencing now, when the wind came up and turned the steam aside—a
geyserite, Taq moment.

It was nearing five now, and I had just enough energy left to
try once more the bend's slowest, deepest pool for its slowest-
rising, fattest fish. A question occurred to me as I was casting (a
cartoonist sketching me at that moment could have traced the
question mark emerging from the top of my floppy hat): what
time in the day had I first come into this world? Eleven in the
morning—wasn't that what my mother used to say? Well, I had
missed it, I'd been trying so hard to fool the trout, and I felt vexed
at that, since it was exactly like seeing your speedometer inch up
to the 100,000 mark, reminding yourself to keep an eye on it to
catch the magic moment, then, a little farther down the highway,
suddenly looking down to see it already at 100,001.

But maybe that's the best way to ease into your fifty-sixth year—a
little blindly, not calibrating the minutes too closely. And perhaps
Mom had said 11:00 p.m.

So, a Muleshoe Bend birthday. The stretch's oddest character-
istic I've not yet mentioned. As immersed as I was in the river's
beauty, as vividly as I took in its wonders, a half hour after leaving
I couldn't help feeling I had made it all up. I have a fairly good
imagination, but I usually know when it's switched on or off.
Fishing the Firehole, I felt like the power had been taken out
of my hands, that I was inside someone else's imagination, a
writer or artist or composer whose powers of invention were a
hell of a lot better than mine are. Perhaps—I wondered later, as
I had a few birthday drinks—it was not me that was imagining
the scene, but the trout who were imagining *me*, that I'm part
of *their* narrative, that I've been fooled by them, hooked, played

and landed. Something wonderful hooked me there, at any rate. Something glorious played me. Something, with a bittersweet little pushing motion, released me back into the drabness in which I usually swim.

Muleshoe gave me a quietly satisfying day, and I followed it with a quietly satisfying evening, beginning with what was virtually a first on my trip: a genuine full-course dinner, and not just anywhere, but at Old Faithful Inn which had recently celebrated its 100th anniversary. Like the feature it was named after, it has the power to make you gasp upon seeing it for the first time. The Gothic lobby of logs and limbs rising ninety feet high; the four-sided fireplace made of five hundred tons of rough-cut local stone; the cozy darkness that takes some getting used to, but, when you do, reveals all kinds of intricate and unexpected western detail. As historian Charles Francis Adams once put it, the inn is "the only man-made structure in the Park that looks as though it grew there." Beloved by generations of visitors, it was very nearly lost during the '88 fires, and you can see by the charred trees that still surround it how close a call this was.

I ordered medallions of elk for dinner, with apologies to the bulls bugling outside, then, remembering it was my birthday, sent my Polish waiter off for a carafe of red wine. Eating alone doesn't particularly bother me, not in a dining room as huge as this one, where you pretty much disappear into the shadowy vastness. There was one terrifying moment when waiters and waitresses approached with a sparkler-lit cake ("How did Celeste arrange that?" I had time to wonder), but they swept on past me and surrounded an older celebrant three tables down.

My notebook had dinner with me, not only to provide some

company, but because I wanted to jot down some resolutions in keeping with the occasion. Profound resolutions would have been nice; there was something about the almost-empty dining room, the candlelight, and the lonely looking waiters (standing by a largely untouched buffet), which made profundity seem like a real possibility. But the most I could come up with were garden-variety resolutions, the kind anyone might make. Pay more attention to friends in the coming year; don't neglect them like I'd been doing. Don't micromanage the kids' lives; draw back a little on the details. Try to avoid turning family life into a matter of small-business administration. Encourage my wife to indulge her love for hiking the way she indulges my passion for fly-fishing. Be there for my father in the trials that will soon be upon him.

I took my time with the wine, took my time with the coffee. Afterward, I wandered across the lobby into the gift shop, but found it disappointing. A Yellowstone gift shop should be unapologetically tacky, gloriously tacky, but I noticed that the stores in the park had gone dramatically upscale since my last visit, selling expensive fleece sweaters or truly wretched western "art." It was difficult, unless you drove out to a gateway town, to find those tacky Yellowstone mugs or shot glasses or pencils that generations of Yellowstone visitors have learned to cherish. I had bought my one personal souvenir on my raid out to West Yellowstone: a 1922 edition of the *Haynes Guide* handbook to Yellowstone that every visitor carried in that era, with a fine engraving of Old Faithful on the cover, charming, evocative old photos, and a detailed guide to what seemed every last geyser in the park. Whoever had owned it had penciled notes in the margins. "Warn Peter about that bear," one said, with intriguing vagueness. Who was Peter and exactly how dangerous was that bear?

I wasn't quite ready to go back to my cabin, so I climbed up to the next level above the lobby and pushed through the massive wooden doors that led to a high porch overlooking Old Faithful. A few older couples were sitting there on benches, and there were two or three of what had become a real rarity that late in autumn—children, one wielding a bow and arrow, ready to protect us if anything rushed us out of the dark. It's pretty automatic to ask when the next eruption is supposed to be, but since everyone got up the moment I came out there, it was obvious that I had just missed it.

No matter. I had some brooding to do which could best be done alone. During my little expedition of one, I had sensed a challenge that I had so far been content to duck. Yellowstone shares a quality with places that have a sadder role in our collective memory—it's the kind of place that tempts you to make solemn pronouncements. It's like Gettysburg or the Flanders trenches in this respect—visiting them, you feel you have to try to understand their meaning, as in, "What is the *meaning* of Gettysburg?" A writer gets modestly paid to modestly ponder, so I felt I had a professional responsibility to take a crack at this, and what better time than now, sitting outside in the sulfurous mist, as alone with Old Faithful and the night as it was possible to be.

What first occurred to me is what Yellowstone is not. Outside Yellowstone, assaulted by the drivel of our times, I often feel like I'm being pelted by a particularly odious kind of sleet and this on what may be an otherwise ordinary day. It feels like not just sleet slamming into my forehead, but every loose and destructive thing the world is capable of hurling. It's sleeting bills and cell phones and telemarketers; it's sleeting junk mail and credit cards and neoconservatives. It's sleeting all the crystallized annoyances and frozen parasites you can think of, and the pellets are so hard, so sharp, so relentless, that the only recourse seems to be to let them, like nails, drive you inch by inch into the ground. In Yellowstone, the sleet stops. There are no malls, no Wal-Marts, no Internet cafes where people chatter on cell phones as they multitask on their computers and watch TV. No traffic jams either, at least not in fall. And while it's unworthy of Yellowstone to sum it up in negatives, such negatives, during your stay in the park, are a very large part of the bliss.

Yellowstone has not escaped history entirely, but it has managed to escape its darkest, bloodiest implications. No battles have ever been fought here—perhaps, given humankind's brutal history, reason enough to celebrate. Yellowstone, whatever else it is, is not Gettysburg, nor is it even the Little Bighorn. The 1877 flight of the Nez Perce from pursuing U.S. Cavalry troops is one of the most needlessly tragic tales in American history, but their detour through the park, to the amazement of startled tourists, had a bumbling, Keystone Kops quality to it, though with sad consequences. Several harmless tourists killed; an old Indian woman or two, too weary to keep up with the others, left alone to die; but the battle that would decide the Nez Perces' fate was fought well to the north. If anything, the flight through the park adds a romantic, colorful chapter to the park's story; when you walk along the Upper Geyser Basin, if you know something about what happened there on August 23, 1877, it's easy to imagine lean, hard warriors emerging from the trees on their horses and yourself with absolutely no place to hide.

Yellowstone had its brush with war—and has been ever since a place one can go in order to forget about war and killing and inhumanity. The chief historical lesson to be taken from Yellowstone is that for once in our tragic and clumsy history we did something right. The motives that led the preservation of these wonders were complicated and not entirely altruistic, but were just virtuous enough to insure passage of the remarkable "Act of Dedication," which established the park on March 1, 1872, whereby Yellowstone was "reserved and withdrawn from settlement, occupancy or sale under the laws of the United States, and dedicated and set aside as a public park or pleasure ground for the benefit and enjoyment of the people."

People did something right here, and if many did something right here, then perhaps humankind is not entirely despicable. That may not be the meaning of Yellowstone, but it's one of the ingredients of its meaning, and goes a long way toward explaining why, more than 130 years later, a visitor from New Hampshire found benefit and enjoyment here, not fear, not sadness, not loathing.

There is a tendency to think that making Yellowstone the country's first national park did the trick, and that the story has been a happy one ever since. But anyone who reads very deeply into the history of the park knows that it has been under constant threat from the day it was established, and faces threats even now. Poachers all but decimated its animal life in the early days; hotels and cabins once sprawled everywhere; plans were floated to flood the wild southwest corner for a reservoir; railroads were kept out only with difficulty.

Today, threats are many. Runaway development pressing in on the park's edges; a gold rush of oil and gas drilling to the southeast; the harm done by snowmobiles, which almost everyone wants out. During my stay, biologists and fly-fishers were just waking up to the fact that there was something seriously wrong with the park's cutthroat trout population—that the Yellowstone Lake cutthroats, one of the world's greatest fisheries, were in serious decline. There seemed to be two reasons for this: the introduction of whirling-disease parasites that often hitch a ride from river to river on an angler's wading boots, and the illegal introduction of lake trout into Yellowstone Lake, a fierce predator that eats everything it can get its greedy jaws on, including juvenile cutthroat trout.

I had experienced this decline myself before anyone admitted it was happening; fishing the Yellowstone River over the course of fifteen years, I'd noticed fewer and fewer fish each visit. That a fisher was responsible for this decline—that an angler had taken lake trout out of Lewis Lake and deliberately dumped them into Yellowstone Lake, not just once, but again and again; that a fisher is responsible for one of the greatest ecological catastrophes in the park's history—did *not* make me feel proud of being an angler. Over the years many people have urged that fishing be banned entirely from national parks, as hunting is banned, and while I can find many good arguments in defense of fishing, this wanton act of vandalism left fly-fishers balancing on very thin moral ice.

It's the twenty-first century we live in; everything we cherish is threatened, almost by definition, and our generation has learned too well what it is to say goodbye to places we love. So, that's part of the Yellowstone meaning, too, the unutterably sad part; if it's beautiful, glorious, enchanting, you can bet your bottom dollar that it is besieged. Enjoy it while it's still here, then. (How often do I hear my friends saying this now, about so many aspects of life.) Love it now—and if that's a cynical message, it's part of Yellowstone's contemporary meaning all the same.

As a novelist, it's my very strong belief that meaning can only be answered on the individual level, and even then, probably inarticulately, in a way that words can't adequately capture. But since

I'm foolish enough to take a stab at it, I'd say that Yellowstone's larger meaning has to do with a quality I wrote about earlier, how by being the oldest unchanged place in America, Yellowstone becomes our youngest place, the place we visit to see what our land was like before we arrived. Walk five minutes from the roads, and you're there again—it's October 11, 1492, and before us spreads the fairest land that ever was or will be again. This is the kind of youth one can experience in Yellowstone—the intoxicating youth of an untarnished dream.

There is another kind of youth you can witness here, on smaller levels, flower by flower, bird by bird, miracle by miracle—the sense, described magnificently by the great American naturalist Henry Beston, "that the creation is still going on, that the creative forces are as great and active today as they have ever been, and that tomorrow morning will be as heroic as any in the world. *Creation is here and now*"—isn't that Yellowstone's meaning in a nutshell? If it is, then doesn't that mean our only possible attitude toward it—and I'm not a man who uses this word lightly—is reverence?

Take Old Faithful, which was gurgling now out there in the darkness, getting ready to repeat for the umpteenth time it's glorious trick. We have known of it for years, it's been visited by millions, used to sell cigarettes and whiskey, drawn and photographed ad infinitum, is the focus of a round-the-clock webcam, and yet, when you walk out to it and stare, what hits you first is the newness, the freshness, the virgin purity of the white cone that surrounds it, the unsullied beauty of its spray. Each eruption could be the first, its wellspring is deep and pure and never-failing, and what it touches in you is the young core that fifty-five years can beat up on, but never quite defeat.

The meaning of Yellowstone? Stir together all these random

thoughts, add your own, and perhaps we can start to come to terms with it, or at least have a good time trying. I hadn't grasped its secret this visit, but maybe I would on the next one, if I learned to watch, think and listen with more care, or if more years brought me more perspective. I walked back down to the lobby, found my way out to my car, drove around the parking lot past the shabby dorms where the waiters and waitresses live, parked outside my humble cabin. This section of the park was in the process of clos-ing down for the season, at least the cabins, and only four were occupied beside mine; our lights in a little semicircle made me realize how it must have been for the soldiers stationed here back in the early 1900s, when the army patrolled the park. The lonely, autumnal mood made it easier to feel fifty-five. "I don't feel any older," is what people say on their birthdays, starting with their fortieth or fiftieth, but if I really examined the issue it was clear that I *did* feel older, and this was coming not so much from any physical changes (though they were there), or any lessening in my imagination (that, at any rate, was strong as ever), but in my entire relationship to time.

That was the big one, far past the mere resolution stage of a typical birthday. At fifty-five our rules of engagement with time are rapidly changing, and already differ significantly from what they were ten years before. No longer does the future spread before you like a blank and wonderful map, yours for the coloring. This is the future my son faces, my daughter. Nor was it critical in the other direction—time wasn't ticking so fast that it froze me into immobility, as it now slowed my father, age eighty-six. It was somewhere in between, but—if I was honest—moving closer and closer to that better-do-it-while-you-can third of the dial, adding an urgency I hadn't felt when I was in my forties.

Take a simple thing like the lavish dinner I had treated myself
to earlier. At forty-five, even at fifty, I might have decided that
it was a luxury I could do without. But now? Well, what was I
waiting for? Why not be nice to myself, I argued; I've earned it,
haven't I? This is one of the turning points that make late middle
age its own unique stage of life; advertisers know this, which is
why you see so many men my age driving brand-new Corvettes.
But the same kind of resolution has a spiritual side. Serenity?
Calmness? Acceptance? All those virtues and strengths you told
yourself you'd grow into someday: if not now, when?

A life is protected by so many milestones and landmarks that it
can seem a fortress that time can't storm. School age looms, first
communion or bar mitzvah, voting age, drinking age, the big 3-0,
the big 4-0, social security eligibility, retirement age—and every
landmark and each birthday forms another barricade protecting
us from old age. And yet the barricades keep falling, and when
fifty-four, like all the others, crumbles into dust, the fifty-five that
replaces it seems to offer very little in the way of shelter, at least
when compared to those solid twenty-fives you sigh for, or even
those rock-hard forty-fours. Each new birthday adds substance
to a person, at least when you're young; but when, I wondered,
does every birthday begin to subtract?

At fifty-five, you begin to play around with the notion of how
much time you actually have left, not to be morbid, but as a real
calculation that influences many different kinds of decisions. Take
my decisions to visit Yellowstone in the autumn, something I had
long wanted to do. *What am I waiting for?* I asked myself that summer. I'd better do this before it's too late. The flip side of this, when
I actually went and did it, was wondering whether I'd ever have the
chance to visit again, or whether this was a farewell tour.

Time would require some thinking about as the year went on, but already I could see other implications in this new relationship. For more years than I could remember, I had been spurred on by the dream of future achievement, not in the go-go, American "success" mode, that old bastard god to whom so many sacrifice their lives, but as an artist who longed for aesthetic success, that rarest of all ambitions. Now, though this still drove me, more and more I was turning from the glittering allure of future achievement to look back at the achievements I had managed, god knows how, to pull off. This was potentially a major switcheroo, and while it wasn't complete yet, I could see a more than subtle part of me preparing for the moment when looking back at the past would seem a more fruitful occupation than dreaming about the future.

As for the increased pace of time, how years go by in a bewildering second now, this was and remained the most surprising fact of adulthood, something that nothing in youth prepared me for. Would it ever level off, or would the pace only increase as I got older?

Though it felt good to have a hefty number of years under my belt now, I wasn't retreating toward nostalgia and reminiscence, not by any means. My past was money in the bank; I felt reassured knowing it was there, but it was an account I wasn't spending from too freely yet—my eyes, for the most part, were still aimed hopefully toward the future.

I'll say it a second time. Late middle age is when the young person in you and the old one stand most tightly back to back. It's why those who seek to recapture their youth seem so foolish to me; so much of your youth is perforce *there*, if not in your face, muscles or looks. Shyness, embarrassment, social terror, overwhelming fury at the foibles of mankind. No one talks about deliberately clinging to these—they cling to you. And the good aspects of youth hardly need restoration. Hope, energy, ambition. By late middle age they've been dinged and dented and generally beat up on, but they're still there, and that's plenty of youth for me. I don't need a twenty-year-old's buff looks, the slick packaging, to feel youth intensely.

And that hope part, that sense of a new beginning. I felt that with particular intensity now. An October birthday is backwards in some respects; it's the month when so much of life begins to grow dormant or die, at least in the Yellowstone mountains, and the bittersweet autumnal mood, with the aspen leaves beginning to fall, is not usually associated with youth. But October suits me this way. It's always been my New Year's, the time of starting over again, my annual jolt of rebirth.

Okay, maybe I wasn't fired up to prove myself anymore career-wise, and I certainly wasn't looking for a mate, didn't feel the need to prove my virility, reproduce myself, spawn. But there were other things I still wanted to do just as vigorously—travel, see more of the world—and that was a young person's ambition in one of its purest forms. Change the world, too. One of the most surprising developments in this aging process was how radical it was making me, so I could see, if this developed along the same curve, dying as a rebel someday, perhaps here in these Yellowstone woods, leading an old-fogy militia of one, hunted down ruthlessly by the authorities for my dissident sensibilities, my small, futile gestures of eco-sabotage.

I'd been reading the work of the essayist A. J. Liebling before I left home, a collection of his reportage from World War Two. The following passage I read three times, after which I put the book down for a thoughtful minute, then read three times more:

Millions of men meriting better than I have lived and died in humiliat-
ing periods of history. Free men and free thinking always get a return
match with the forces of sadism and anti-reason. But I had wanted
to see a win. I had wanted my era to be one of those that read well in
books. Some people like to live in a good neighborhood; I like to live
in a good age.

My condition is just the opposite of Liebling's — I live in a good
neighborhood, but in a bad age, where the forces of sadism, anti-
reason, hubris and greed are fully in the saddle and ride our backs.
Rereading this passage, I realized how much I yearn for this
myself; just for once, in this sordid age, to witness and be part of
a happy ending that will someday read well in a book, and to live
long enough to buy that book myself, read about how people — just
when things looked darkest — managed by luck and by courage
not only to survive but also to take a resolute step forward toward
a new golden age, or at least a reasonably shiny bronze one.

Other than that disappointment, I was feeling pretty good about
things now. I could see lots of advantages in getting up there, as
for instance all the meaningless social obligations and routine
chores I could duck using my age as an excuse, as in "Oh, I'm too
old for that now," which, to my own surprise and amusement,
I'd begun saying more frequently the past year, never having
said it once before. Too old to worry about what people think of
me; too old to do things merely for appearances' sake; too old to
keep up to date on who the hottest celebrities are; too old for the
latest inventions.

In that sense, late middle age is liberation from the pettiness
of life, or at least it should be — a sneak preview of the greater

liberation that death will someday bring. "A good man," Thackeray once wrote, "grows simpler as he grows older," and that was certainly one of my ambitions—and yet what was interesting was that I should feel this quintessentially old man's ambition with all the fierce longing of youth.

When do these two conjoined halves finally separate, the old person in you become distanced from the child? When, in other words, does late middle age end? Well, probably not at fifty-six, that's the good news. Not, I suspect, at sixty-six either. With increased life spans, seniors running wild, who's to say when the younger person becomes so remote in you that there is no summoning him or her back? Late middle age is a stage of life I'm enjoying to the maximum, and ten more years of it would be nice. Twenty more years would be even nicer.

For three weeks I had been able to escape the responsibilities and obligations waiting to tug me back from my solitary mood. But these existed—fifty-six wasn't going to be any different in this respect from fifty-five. I'd done a lot of thinking over the last year, had approached the mystery of life's middle stage just closely enough to know that if you're the type to fool around with such matters, you can't expect your answers to be definite. My philosophy could be reduced to a few basic words—courage, love, nature, art—and in the simplifying mood I was in, it seemed just enough to pronounce these silently to myself; they were part of me now—I didn't have to torture myself with long explanations of why they were important as I did when I was younger. They formed—in my imaginings, in my everyday life—a barrier of protective hills, inside of which was locked a precious vale, one I was scarcely fit to inhabit myself, what with my middle-age busyness and irritability, but one I could dream of someday entering.

Yes, there is a secret to life, a thousand secrets, and yes, there are keys that might unlock them, the ones I've written about here, which, though I live to be a hundred, will remain the only keys I know.

I wrote down a few thoughts on these subjects, knowing even as I did so that they were the kind I'd probably scratch out first thing next morning. Then I remembered that before I had left on my trip, everyone in my family had written cards for me, not to be opened until my actual birthday, and that I'd stashed them at the bottom of my duffle bag with my extra fly reels. Celeste's note was short and sweet, and contained one line that got me smiling. "Remember, the fish *like* you" — and yes, this was true; any time I felt down or homesick, the trout had all but sprung from the water to pat me fraternally on the back. Matthew's was a soccer puzzle; by filling in the blank letters in various soccer stars' names, I ended up with the words "I love you."

The longest letter was Erin's, and this is the one that shook me deep and hard, so as I finished it, lying there on the bed in the soft light of my table lamp, I began unashamedly to cry.

> *Hi Dad! I hope you're having a good time, and that you're not getting too comfortable without us! It must be nice just to get away some times from all the arguing and complaining and stress. Do you ever learn things you didn't know about yourself on solo trips, or when you're by yourself? You seem to want to be alone a lot, but maybe that's the writer in you. I'm still learning stuff about myself, but that's to be expected. Umm . . . Please remember that I am as scared/excited about going to college as you are about me going. It will be easier if we both know that.*

I hope you have a good 55th birthday and make sure to eat a bison burger and a Montana Monster cookie for me! Happy birthday, love Erin!

Throughout my stay in the park I carried around in my head, the way you do a catchy jingle, an idea for a novel. Writers are always doing this, of course. This particular idea was the harmless, non-tormenting kind that probably wouldn't ever lead to much, but was fun to roll around in my imagination. There's an opening here, a need: Yellowstone has never been the subject of a great book. The hero would be a man my age or slightly younger, who, acting on a whim, never having been there before, decides to visit the park just before something calamitous shakes the world—9/11 say, or the start of the Iraq war. He immediately becomes fascinated, falls in love as he's never fallen in love with a place before, its beauty, its peacefulness, even its primness (and, yes, Yellowstone, wild as it is, has its prim side). So deep is this enchantment and so bad is the news in the outside world that he can't bring himself to leave when his allotted time is up. He extends his reservation, e-mails some excuse to his wife, and keeps staying on and on right through the summer and then the fall. He would have an affair of course—maybe with one of those woman rangers who now seem to outnumber the men—and between this and his adventures in the backcountry, comes face to face with what the reviewers (unanimous in their praise) call his "essential core values." As winter comes, he's taking a job as a dishwasher in one of the park lodges just to keep the connection going—or should I give him a fatal disease, have him crawl off to die in an empty beaver lodge as epiphanic snow falls down?

An autobiographical novel? Well, partly. I had become just as enchanted by Yellowstone as my hero; and, yes, I hated ferociously to leave. (The shortest sentence in John Muir's rapturously lyrical essay on Yellowstone is the following: "It is a hard place to leave.") But unlike my hero, I had strong ties pulling me out from the enchanted zone, bonds, that if you looked at them correctly, were just as wondrous themselves.

I had done okay during my three weeks — I had done okay. I learned that I still have the stamina to fish hard, learned that my eyes were still quick enough to respond to a trout's subtle rise, that my reflexes were still fast enough to enjoy this kind of big-league fly-fishing. I remembered enough about tenderness that releasing trout carefully was still a big priority; only my children when they were babies ever got the TLC I lavished on that big Soda Butte cutthroat or that fat Madison brown. I discovered that I could still take care of myself alone, not only in the backcountry, but in that wilder jungle of airports, highways and motels — learned that traveling alone makes you filter everything through the screen of your own seeing, with no compromises blurring things. I had reconnected with the boy in me — not just through fishing, but through my renewed willingness to sit, watch and wonder. Yellowstone had once again given me an unsurpassable standard by which to measure beauty, wildness, perfection. It had supplied me with a deep reservoir of solace to help me through the coming year.

A good trip. A good life to match? Well, I could total that up, too, while I was at it. At fifty-five, I still had my health and three-fourths of my energy. I still had my curiosity. I was still trying to puzzle things out. I still had a surprisingly high number of traits left from youth, the bedrock fears, inclinations, and attitudes that apparently one never totally leaves behind; even a good deal of innocence remains, which one would think would be the first quality to go. I was still asking a lot of myself, asking a lot from life in general. As for the demerits, the down side, virtues I had lost, places where I'd better improve quick—

They could wait. It was my birthday plus one. I was entering this fifty-five business slowly, and one of my resolutions, jotted down as the final entry in my notebook, was to give that oh-so-serious side of me a little more vacation.

I'll say it for a second time. Alone, I'd done okay. But the biggest lesson to take home, along with the souvenir mugs and T-shirts, was the fact that I wasn't alone, not in any sense short of the ultimate metaphysical one. Any definition I could come up with about who I was on this landmark birthday involved my being a husband, a father, a son; these connections were real and vital, and—the first two coming late in life—all but miraculous. And demanding. I can't pretend it wasn't welcome, a vacation from being chauffeur, tutor, dishwasher, cook, but if I had any illusions that the true me was a solo me, the painful wave of homesickness that washed over me on my last night proved otherwise.

On my first trip to Yellowstone in 1988, the plane ride home had taken me right over the park, which was invisible except for one monstrously large cloud of red-veined blackness, a cloud that, for all anyone knew at the time, was erasing the beauty of Yellowstone for an entire generation. It hadn't managed to do this, of course. Fire had renewed its beauty—and I saw it now, as our flight took the same shortcut mine had fifteen years before, slanting high across Yellowstone Lake. That early in the morning, the cold tightened and showcased all the hot springs and geysers within the enormous caldera, so that the park seemed the base for a thousand columns of the lightest, most ethereal gray imaginable, holding up the sky.

I watched these for as long as I could, twisting around in my seat to look out the window behind me, then turned with the greatest reluctance away. People were donning headphones now, taking out laptops, unwrapping their breakfast bars and peanuts. My thoughts turned eastward as the plane did too. The birthday boy had done okay in Wonderland—and come another year closer to the man he was meant to be.

In the American Lives series

Turning Bones
by Lee Martin

Between Panic and Desire
by Dinty W. Moore

Thoughts from a Queen-Sized Bed
by Mimi Schwartz

The Fortune Teller's Kiss
by Brenda Serotte

Gang of One
Memoirs of a Red Guard
by Fan Shen

Just Breathe Normally
by Peggy Shumaker

Scraping By in the Big Eighties
by Natalia Rachel Singer

In the Shadow of Memory
by Floyd Skloot

Secret Frequencies
A New York Education
by John Skoyles

Phantom Limb
by Janet Sternburg

Yellowstone Autumn
A Season of Discovery in a Wondrous Land
by W. D. Wetherell

Books by W. D. Wetherell

Souvenirs (Random House, 1981)

Vermont River (Winchester, 1984)

The Man Who Loved Levittown (Pittsburgh, 1985)

Hyannis Boat and Other Stories (Little, Brown, 1989)

Chekhov's Sister (Little, Brown, 1990)

Upland Stream (Little, Brown, 1991)

The Wisest Man in America (New England, 1995)

The Smithsonian Guides to Natural America:
Northern New England (Smithsonian, 1995)

Wherever That Great Heart May Be (New England, 1996)

North of Now (Lyons, 1998)

One River More (Lyons, 1998)

Small Mountains (Tenna Nova, 2000)

Morning (Pantheon, 2001)

This American River (New England, 2002)

A Century of November (Michigan, 2004)

Soccer Dad (Skyhorse, 2008)